Messianic Discipleship

Following Yeshua,
Growing in Messiah

Sam Nadler

"Messianic Discipleship: Following Yeshua, Growing in Messiah"
by Sam Nadler
Printed in the United States of America
2014th Edition (v.1.0)

Shalom, my friend!

Though "discipleship," dry as that word is, may not conjure up Pacific island breezes or dancing *Hasidim*, it should be a clarion call to growth and maturity in relating to the God of Israel. Unlike many books on the subject, this book seeks to introduce *talmidut*, or discipleship from a Biblically Jewish frame of reference.

Not only are the Scriptures essentially Jewish, but it is the revelation of God in Messiah. He is the *Aleph* and the *Tav*, the First and the Last. Yeshua is Jewish, *and* He is the Truth incarnate. So as you grow in a Messianic frame of reference, we hope that this book will help you appreciate more deeply the love of HaShem.

The books *Following Yeshua* and *Growing in Messiah* have been used for over a decade to lead Jewish and Gentile believers through the core issues of faith in Yeshua. Since the issues covered in those works dovetailed together, we saw a need to combine them into one. As expected, some facets also needed updating along the way. We are excited to offer the result of those efforts, *Messianic Discipleship*.

I am grateful to many people including: Moishe Rosen, who had me memorize Scripture as a brand new believer; my wonderful wife Miriam, as well as proofreaders Ann Thomas, Pat Campbell, Shari Belfer, and the many more who have made suggestions and corrections, even while being discipled through this material; Natalia Fomin for the genesis of the idea to combine the books; and finally, my son Matt who oversaw and edited the project.

The format of the teaching is to have the student determine the answers from the actual Scripture being studied. This will provide a direct understanding of what the Bible teaches, and allow enjoyment of the truth of God's word for the student. May this book be used to train up many more, and may even more of our people recognize and turn to Messiah because of *your* studies in this book!

Sam Nadler

Table of Contents

Note: The four parts of this book are marked by the first four letters of the Hebrew *aleph-bet*. They are pronounced:

    aleph

    bet

    gimel

    dalet

Traditionally, Hebrew letters can double as numbers (for example, to number chapters in a book of the Bible). So, *aleph* = 1, *bet* (or *vet*) = 2, *gimel* = 3, *dalet* = 4.

PART 1

New Identity

Lesson 1

Getting Started

Mazel Tov! Welcome to the challenging, all-encompassing, life-transforming journey of following Yeshua. If you are entering into this process it is because **you are a child of God by faith in Yeshua!**

"Faith" simply means belief, trust, dependence, or reliance upon Yeshua, God's promised Messiah. The Scriptures teach that God has always accepted people through faith in Him. Such was the case when Abraham believed God's word, and the Lord accepted him:

> *And he [Abraham] believed the* LORD*; and the* LORD *deemed it to him as righteousness (Genesis 15:6).*

A right relationship with God was never based on merely being Jewish, or even keeping the *mitzvot* (the commandments), such as *Brit Milah* (circumcision).

> *"Behold, the days are coming," says the* LORD*, "that I will punish all who are circumcised with the uncircumcised—Egypt, Judah, Edom, the people of Ammon, Moab, and all who are in the farthest corners, who dwell in the wilderness. For all these nations are uncircumcised, and all the house of Israel are uncircumcised in the heart." (Jeremiah 9:25-26)*

God always wanted His people to have a heart relationship with Him by faith. The New Covenant declares the same results of faith in God for everyone who believes in Yeshua the Messiah, *Ben Elohim*, God's Son.

In John 3:16, the Scripture states:

> *"For God so loved the world that He gave His only Son, in order that everyone who believes in Him should not perish but have eternal life."*

If you are not familiar with this verse, please carefully read it again. According to John 3:16, for what reason did God give His only Son?

"For God so _____ the world."

This is always the motive of God's heart: Love! And this should be the motive of your heart as you relate and trust in the Lord.

According to John 3:16, what was God's purpose in giving His only Son, Yeshua?

"In order that everyone...should not _____ but have _____ _____."

According to John 3:16, who are those that are promised not to perish (that is, be condemned to judgment), but rather to have eternal life?

"Everyone who _____ in Him."

Please read John 3:16 again but this time instead of where it says the world, say "me," and instead of everyone, say "I." Try it!

"Because God so loved ___ _____ that He gave His only Son, in order that _____ who believes in Him, should not perish but have eternal life."

Personalizing the Scriptures can help us see how God's Word is personally meaningful. God's Word can be compared with a love letter. It is for you, and all who trust in the God of Israel.

For example, the verse above shows that if you have come to believe in Yeshua, you have eternal life (this is discussed in Lesson 2). Like Abraham and everyone who has put his trust in God and His promises, you also have personally trusted in God's promised Messiah, Yeshua. Thus, Yeshua said, *"Your ancestor Abraham rejoiced to see My day, and he saw it and was glad" (John 8:56).*

To trust in Yeshua is to believe in the God of Israel even as Abraham, King David, and all the prophets of Israel believed. By faith in Messiah Yeshua, you have accepted the Biblical way of salvation which is not only for Jews, but for all who will believe. Yes, He is Savior for the whole world, as well as Israel's Messiah!

Those who trust in Yeshua have new life, a new relationship with God, and a new way of looking at the world. Still, there are also many practical issues that need to be handled in a manner pleasing to God, and spiritual truths that need to be understood and enjoyed by all believers. The process of working through, handling, and understanding these matters is called discipleship.

Why Discipleship Matters

The concept "discipleship" comes from the Hebrew *hanakh*, which means "to make narrow, dedicate, train" (from this word we get the holiday Hanukkah, the Feast of Dedication). Even as the Hebrew Scriptures tell us to be dedicated or discipled servants and sons, so our Messiah expects all believers to be involved in discipleship and nurtured in His word (Genesis 14:14; Proverbs 22:6).

> *"Go therefore and make disciples of all the nations, immersing them in the name of the Father and of the Son and of the Holy Spirit, teaching them to observe all the things that I have commanded you; and lo, I am with you always, even to the end of the age" (Matthew 28:19-20).*

This portion is commonly called the Great Commission. Messiah has commissioned us in a great work which He has prepared. In other words, we are trained so that we can train others.

Discipleship enables new believers to:

✡ grow in their relationship with God;

✡ develop spiritual understanding of the truths of God's Word;

✡ gain wisdom for living faithfully for the Lord; and

✡ have fellowship with other believers.

By faith in Yeshua, you are made God's child; by discipleship, you mature as His child. By faith, you are saved from eternal judgment; by discipleship, you grow with respect to that salvation. Just as there is no salvation without faith in Yeshua, so also there is no spiritual growth without discipleship.

The discipleship process spiritually stabilizes the believer in the faith; undiscipled believers are the "wandering Jews" of the body of Messiah.

> *We should no longer be children, tossed to and fro and carried about with every wind of doctrine...but, speaking the truth in love, we grow up in all things into Him who is the head—Messiah (Ephesians 4:14-15).*

There is a starting point and an ending point to this process. It should begin once you have placed your faith in Yeshua as Messiah, Lord and Savior. It ends when we arrive in heaven, where *"we will know as we've been known" (1 Corinthians 13:12)*. Get ready for the journey of growing in His love and life!

Lesson 2

Your Identity in Messiah

The God of Israel wants you to have a deep assurance that by faith in Yeshua you are His child forever. This means you are:

1. Forgiven

2. Saved

3. Have eternal life

    ...and if you were born Jewish...

4. You are <u>still</u> Jewish!

1. You are Forgiven

You are forgiven for all your sins through Messiah's atonement (you have peace with God and are in a right and loving relationship with Him). This is just what the Hebrew Scriptures promised: that Messiah would come and die for our sins as God's provision for our atonement and forgiveness.

> *But He was wounded for our transgressions, crushed for our iniquities; upon Him was the punishment that made us whole, and by His bruises we are healed. All we like sheep have gone astray; we have all turned to our own way, and the LORD has laid on Him the iniquity of us all (Isaiah 53:5-6).*

If you are not familiar with this section of Scripture, take a moment to read the entire portion of Isaiah 52:13-53:12 (in Appendix B). The New Covenant shows how God fulfilled this promise of redemption. Please read:

> *Therefore, having been justified by faith, we have peace with God through our Lord Yeshua the Messiah (Romans 5:1).*

The word "justified" means: to be declared righteous, or to have a right standing before God. Because Messiah has fully atoned for your sins, you are now completely forgiven and spiritually spotless before God. As it says in Psalm 32:1:

Blessed is he whose transgression is forgiven, whose sin is covered.

According to Romans 5:1 (on p. 11), how is someone justified or forgiven before God?

"By _____".

That's correct: by faith. That is, by simple trust in Messiah you are justified. "Peace with God" means that we are no longer under His wrath, but instead we experience His mercy and blessing. The Lord has a peaceful and harmonious relationship with the person who has faith in Yeshua.

Do you have faith in Yeshua?

Yes_____ No _____

If you checked "Yes," then you are j_____ and forgiven, and you have p_____ with God. At this time, please read Romans 5:1 replacing we and our with I and my.

"Therefore, having been justified by faith, _____ have peace with God through _____ Lord Yeshua the Messiah."

2. You are Saved

In Messiah, you are completely delivered from all judgment for your sins. This is the same truth anticipated in Isaiah 45:22:

"Look to Me, and be saved, all you ends of the earth! For I am God, and there is no other."

As we might think of a fireman who goes into a burning building to save someone from a fire, so the Messiah underwent judgment to save us from the fires of judgment.

The idea of being saved is to be delivered from judgment for our sins, and placed into the family of God.

Please read:

> *If you confess with your mouth the Lord Yeshua and believe in your*
> *heart that God has raised Him from the dead, you will be saved*
> *(Romans 10:9).*

The word confess in the original language (*homologeo*) means liter
ally "same-word," that is, to agree with another. We agree with God
about Yeshua. So, to confess with your mouth means to acknowledge Yeshua as *Adonai* (Lord). Real faith is evidenced in what we
confess as true.

Is this what you acknowledge as well?

Yes_____ No _____

The word believe is synonymous with trust, depend and rely upon;
as opposed to mere intellectual assent. We trust the Scriptures, God's
testimony and promises regarding our salvation. To believe in your
heart that God has raised Him from the dead means you genuinely
trust that through the resurrection of Messiah, God glorified Yeshua
and accepted His righteous death as atonement for your sins.

Is this what you genuinely believe?

Yes_____ No _____

According to Romans 10:9, what is the guarantee for all who confess
and believe? _____ _____ _____ _____.

Therefore, since you confess and believe, what are you also guaranteed in Romans 10:9? _____ _____ _____ _____

Please read Romans 10:9, replacing "I" and "my" for the words "you"
and "your."

"If _____ confess with _____ mouth the Lord Yeshua and
believe in _____ heart that God has raised Him from the
dead, ___ will be saved!"

3. You have Eternal Life now!

This means God's life dwells in you, now and forever. This is the same truth our people anticipated in Deuteronomy 30:6:

> *"And the LORD your God will circumcise your heart and the heart of your descendants, to love the LORD your God with all your heart and with all your soul, that you may live."*

Read the following verse:

> *"These things I have written to you who believe in the name of the Son of God, so that you may know that you have eternal life." (1 John 5:13, NASB)*

According to 1 John 5:13, to whom was it written?

_____.

The word "that" indicates purpose. According to 1 John 5:13, why was it written?

_____

_____.

Therefore, since you also believe in the name of the Son of God what do you know you have? _____

_____.

Please read 1 John 5:13 again placing your name for the word you.

> "These things I have written to _____ who believe(s) in the name of the Son of God, that _____ may know that _____ has eternal life" (1 John 5:13).

4. You are still Jewish!

This must be stressed because there are some who falsely teach that Jewish people who believe in Yeshua stop being Jewish. The New Covenant Scriptures do not teach that a Jewish person who believes in Yeshua becomes an ex-Jew or a non-Jew. (By the way, if you were not born Jewish, then you are still a Gentile, seen in Romans 11:13, but connected to Israel through the Messiah of Israel, seen in Ruth 1:16. So, as a Messianic Gentile, welcome to the family, and keep reading.)

Notice what Paul, the Apostle, says about himself many years after coming to faith in Yeshua: *"Paul replied, 'I am a Jew, from Tarsus'"* *(Acts 21:39; see also, Acts 22:3).*

He also wrote to a mostly non-Jewish congregation in Rome:

I ask, then, has God rejected his people? By no means! Because I am an Israelite, a descendant of Abraham, a member of the tribe of Benjamin. (Romans 11:1)

In these Scriptures, Paul declares "I am a Jew" and "I am an Israelite." Is this something that only used to be true, will be true in the future, or is now true? Consider the tense of the verb. Is the tense of the verb "am" past, present, or future?

It is in the _____ tense.

Now, unlike Paul, you may not be from the city of Tarsus, or from the tribe of Benjamin, but according to Scripture, if either parent is Jewish, then you are also Jewish.

Paul was not only still Jewish, but unashamed to say so to both Gentiles and his own Jewish people. It was not that being Jewish gave him any merit before God. On the contrary, Paul knew all his merit, or righteousness, was found in Yeshua alone (Philippians 3:8-9; Ephesians 1:3). Yet, from Paul's comments in Romans 11, it is obvious that he was Jewish in the present tense. If you are Jewish, you are to be a "present tense" Jewish person, also.

Though every spiritual blessing in heaven is found in Yeshua Himself, your Jewishness is an ongoing testimony that God is faithful (Romans 11:1). God does not change. He would never forsake the Jews or annul them as a people (Jeremiah 31:35-37). This testimony matters, not because of what we have done, or who we are, but because of what *Messiah* has done. Though we have fallen short of God's glory, we can boast in His faithfulness (Romans 3:23).

While it is true that at the present time the majority of believers in Yeshua are Gentiles - a fact we celebrate! - Yeshua is truly the Jewish Messiah. Faith in Yeshua cannot make Jews into Gentiles.

Allow me to illustrate this idea with a story about a Jewish restaurant (the Bible), the food it served (Yeshua, 'the Bread of Life', John 6:35), and the mostly Gentile neighborhood where it was located (the world). If this Jewish restaurant served such great food that many Gentiles became patrons of the restaurant, would that make the food non-Jewish? Of course not! Jews could still eat there and enjoy "home cooking."

Let's say those same Gentile patrons enjoyed the food so much that they took some home in their own non-Jewish containers. This still wouldn't alter anything about the food in the restaurant being Jewish. And Jews who continue eating in that restaurant would not stop being Jewish.

The irony is this: at first some of the Jewish customers thought that any Gentile patron of such a Jewish restaurant had to become Jewish! In fact, it became a real controversy for the Jewish restaurant, so much so, that all of the original Jewish patrons came together to discuss this issue. It was finally decided that Gentiles who eat Jewish food don't become Jewish, just fulfilled Gentiles (you can read of the actual controversy and decision in Acts 15).

God, the Father, did not send Messiah to make Gentiles into Jews, or Jews into Gentiles, but to make all people His children, and a spiritual family by faith in Yeshua. God's desire for Gentiles as well as Jewish people is that they trust in Israel's Messiah. In Him, Jews and Gentiles can have unity without uniformity.

Indeed He says, "It is too small a thing that You should be My Ser-

vant to raise up the tribes of Jacob, and to restore the preserved ones of Israel; I will also give You as a light to the Gentiles, that You should be My salvation to the ends of the earth." (Isaiah 49:6)

Even as the Scriptures assure you that Yeshua is the Messiah, the Scriptures are clear that Messiah came to be God's Servant for salvation and light to the Gentiles, as well as to Israel.

Your salvation and everyone else's as well comes from trusting in Yeshua for atonement and new life, just as the Older Covenant prophesied and is fulfilled in the New Covenant.

Your assurance of eternal salvation comes from God's unchanging Word. You can have full confidence that God fully accepts you and all who come to Him through Messiah Yeshua.

Please read the following scriptures regarding assurance of your salvation: John 6:35-40; 10:27-30; Romans 8:28-39.

Please memorize these verses:

Romans 5:1 –

Romans 10:9 –

1 John 5:13 –

In addition, please write out a paragraph on how you know you are saved, using the Scriptures from this chapter.

_____

_____

_____

_____

_____

_____

_____

_____

_____

_____

PART 2

Relational Habits

Lesson 3

Prayer

Baruch HaShem! Blessed be the Name! You are a *yeled shel Elohim*, a child of God forever by faith in Yeshua. You have eternal life and an eternal relationship with the Lord God of Israel through His Messiah. As with all children and relationships, there needs to be growth and maturity. As you spiritually mature in your faith, you will develop an even more intimate and fulfilling relationship with the Lord.

How does a believer spiritually grow in the faith? There are four essential areas that need to become more and more a vital part of our daily lives: prayer, reading the Scriptures, fellowship, and sharing our faith.

These four areas will cover the two basic directions of your spiritual growth: the vertical (with God) and horizontal (with people). Prayer and scripture will address the vertical relationship between you and the Lord. Fellowship and sharing will focus on the horizontal relationships between you and other people.

Spiritual growth and balance come from prioritizing all four of these values. Those missing any of these habits can become like spiritual nerds, having a "speciality," but without balance or maturity. None of the areas can be outgrown, but rather we grow deeper in them as we walk more closely with the Lord.

The goal of this section is to help you develop a prayer life: a daily, ongoing, intimate time to speak with your Heavenly Father. Though some of us grew up chanting beautiful liturgical prayers and praise, prayer is essentially and most importantly "talking with God." Setting aside even five minutes a day to talk with *Abba* (Father) can make all the difference in the world.

The Psalms are actually prayers and praise to God.

I will cry out to God Most High, to God who accomplishes all things for me (Psalm 57:2[3]).

King David authored 73 of the 150 psalms. David was thankful that he could "cry out" to God. In Hebrew, *karah* actually means "to cry or call out loudly." This teaches us that private prayer is not to be merely formalistic, but sincere, or with *kavanah* (intention).

We can genuinely express to God our feelings, thoughts, frustrations, will, or concerns about any matter. God can take it; He won't be offended or shocked. He actually desires and expects an open relationship with us. When we are real with God, we receive real help from God: comfort for our pain, encouragement in our disappointments, power for our weaknesses, renewed love when we are resentful, and forgiveness when we stumble. The New Covenant reiterates this truth:

> *...casting all your worries upon Him, for He cares for you*
> *(1 Peter 5:7).*

God cares about our lives and can help us in the midst of difficulty. Because of our relationship with God, we have freedom in our prayer life to totally give all our burdens to the One who really loves us.

In Psalm 57:2, David's confidence was not only that God would hear his deepest cry, but also that God would accomplish all things for him. All believers in Messiah can have this same confidence. Yeshua said, *"If you ask anything in My name, I will do it"* (John 14:14). Asking in His name is not some magical phrase, but it means asking in His authority, for His reputation and honor, and in light of His purposes and will as revealed in the Scriptures. He will accomplish all things for you that are good, wholesome, wise, and according to His purposes for your life.

God always answers prayer; however, His answer may be...

✡ "Yes" (because it is appropriate for you now),

✡ "Not at this time" or "Wait" (because it may only be appropriate for you at a future time), or

✡ "No" (because it is inappropriate for you at any time).

We trust in His power to provide, but also in His wisdom to provide that which is in our eternal best interests. Please read these next verses.

> *Now this is the confidence that we have in Him, that if we ask any-thing according to His will, He hears us. And if we know that He hears us – whatever we ask – we know that we have the petitions that we have asked of Him (1 John 5:14-15).*

What does it mean that "He hears us"? The writer means that God does not ignore us; if we ask according to what is His plan for us, He will fulfill our request. So according to 1 John 5:14-15, how can you be confident that He hears you?

_____

_____

The key to our prayer life and our requests of God is to know His _____. But how can we know His will? God's Word, the Scrip-tures, is the revealed will of God. As we come to know His Word, we learn His will, desires, and concerns for us. We better understand God's character, values, priorities, and His perspective on life.

Please read 1 John 5:14-15 again, this time replacing we and us, with "I" and "me."

> "Now this is the confidence that __ have in Him, that if __ ask anything according to His will, He hears ___. And if __ know that He hears ___, whatever __ ask, __ know that __ have the petitions that __ have asked of Him."

Now please read this next verse:

> *If I regard wickedness in my heart, the Lord will not hear (Psalm 66:18).*

Since God knows all things (this is called "omniscience"), we know He always hears us. In this verse, the phrase "will not hear" refers to the Lord not responding positively to our requests. The

Hebrew word for regard is *rayiti*, which means "to consider" or "gaze at." If we desire something evil or improper for ourselves or others, it is just plain wrong. The Lord will not hear or respond to evil.

According to Psalm 66:18, where do you regard (or consider) good or evil? ____ ____ _____.

Yes, in your heart. Let us understand the *internal* priorities of prayer. Regardless of what we say with our lips, it is the inner person that spiritually communes with the Lord. *External* expressions of prayer are so others can join with us in prayer and praise to God.

What specific sins or wickedness may possibly be in your heart in the following areas?

* Personal life?
* Family life?
* Financial or business areas?
* Community life?

After thinking about these areas, did you find some that you are not pleased with? What can you do about the sins or wickedness in your heart? Consider 1 John 1:9:

> *If we confess our sins, [God] is faithful and just to forgive us our sins and to cleanse us from <u>all</u> unrighteousness.*

"Confess" in the original Greek language is *homologeo* ("same word"). This means "to agree with another" - in this case, with God. In other words, when we admit or confess to God our sins or wickedness we are finally agreeing with Him about what He already knows — that our sinful thoughts, attitudes, or deeds are unjustifiable, but not unforgivable.

What is done in the heart only is a sin against God and must be confessed. If you sin outwardly, you are sinning against God and others. You need to confess your sins in either case: often to the person against whom you have sinned, as well as to the Lord, as all sin is rebellion against Him (Matthew 5:22-25; 18:15; James 5:16).

Rather than the sin being clever, cute or a matter of "he started it," sin is contrary to God's character and revealed will in the Scriptures. We can truly praise God, because when we admit our thoughts or deeds as sinful, He forgives and cleanses us in Messiah's atonement!

When I recognize wickedness in my heart, what am I, as a believer in Yeshua, to do? (Pick one)

___ 1.) I am to be proud that I can sin in my heart and it doesn't matter.

___ 2.) I am to beat myself up for being such a sinful loser.

___ 3.) I am to confess it to God as sin and accept His atonement in Messiah.

___ 4.) I am to see if there is a market for this particular sin, then mass produce it.

(The answer, if you are wondering, is 3.)

Personalize 1 John 1:9 using "I", "my" and "me".

"If ___ confess ___ sins, He is faithful and just to forgive ___ ___ sins and to cleanse ___ from all unrighteousness."

For further reading on prayer, read Exodus 33:12-19, the Psalms, and John 17.

Please memorize:

1 John 1:9 –

Psalm 66:18 –

Please commit yourself to begin a minimum of five minutes of daily prayer. Make it at a time when you are awake, alone, and able to quiet your thoughts before God. If you are not sure how to structure your prayer time, a help for many believers is the acronym "ACTS"

Adoration — appreciate the worthiness of God, His attributes, love and goodness. Then, in light of Who He is,

Confession -- we confess our sins and failings before Him. Next,

Thanksgiving -- take time to thank the Lord for His forgiveness, cleansing, and many blessings of Messiah in your life. Finally, make

Supplication -- requests before Him, asking Him to supply your needs as well as the needs of others.

Take time each day also to be quiet before the Lord. That way, He gets to minister to your heart as *Ruach HaKodesh* (the Holy Spirit) uses the Word of God to remind you of His great love for you!

Prayer is the means believers have to talk to the Holy One of Israel - what a privilege!

Lesson 4

Scripture

We have considered the issue of prayer, which is us talking to God. Scripture is God's way of speaking to us. The Scriptures are composed of the *Tanakh* (or Old Covenant) and the *Brit Chadashah* (New Covenant).

✡ *Tanakh* (pronounced ta-*nakh*) is a traditional Hebrew acrostic for *Torah* (the Law), *Nevi'im* (the Prophets), and *Ketuvim* (the Writings). These are the texts which anticipate the coming of Messiah.

✡ *Brit Chadashah* (pronounced be-*reet* cha-da-*sha*) are the writings of the Apostles, those immediate disciples of Yeshua who were authorized to give His truth. In many circles this is called the "New Testament" (as Testament is another word for Covenant).

The *Tanakh* is God's promise of life. The New Covenant is the fulfillment of that promise. The Scripture is reliable in all it asserts about life, both temporal (on earth) and eternal (in heaven).

Please read the following scripture:

Every word of God is pure; He is a shield to those who put their trust in Him (Proverbs 30:5).

The word for pure in the Hebrew is *tserufah*, meaning to "make or prove <u>true</u> through refining." God's Word is tested and found to be eternally true and pure (without error). In the verse above, how much of God's word is pure or proven true?

_____.

The Scripture reveals that every word of God is completely reliable. The word every in Hebrew is *kol*, meaning every or all. Therefore, it is a totally trustworthy testimony of God and His priorities.

According to Proverbs 30:5, what is a believer guaranteed if they trust in Him (that is, believe in His word)?

_____

Yes, "He is a shield to those who trust in Him" and his Word. A shield is protection against an attack from the enemy. The safest place to be is in God's will, and God's Word is His revealed will for you. Thus, as you trust and follow His Word, the Scriptures, you are in His will and shielded from the enemy. Consider now this verse:

> *Your Word I have hidden in my heart, that I might not sin against You (Psalm 119:11).*

The Hebrew word for "hidden" (*tsafan*) means "to hide, treasure or store up". The practical application of having God's Word hidden in my heart is memorizing, personalizing, trusting and following the Scriptures. According to Psalm 119:11, what is the result of having God's Word hidden (or treasured) in your heart?

_____

When we treasure and obey His Word, He enables and enlightens us to follow and not rebel against Him. The way to keep from sinning against the Lord and to please Him is to follow His Word.

Having His Word in your heart is to have the Word deep within your being: in the place where you make decisions and choices to either trust and follow the Lord or not. Please read this next verse:

> *To the law and to the testimony! If they do not speak according to this Word, it is because there is no light in them (Isaiah 8:20).*

According to this verse, where should you turn to for truth?

_____

Yes, to the law and to the testimony, God's word. The law and the testimony refers to the Scriptures, or God's Word. The law or *torah* means "instruction" (literally, "what is pointed out"): essentially, authoritative instruction. The word testimony, *te'udah*, is used in reference to the tablets of the Ten Commandments (Exodus 31:18, etc.), as well as referring to the ark in the Tabernacle that contained the Ten Commandments (Ex. 40:21).

As the Psalmist wrote, *"the testimony of the LORD is sure" (Psalm 19:7)*. God's Word is His authoritative and fully trustworthy testimony of what is always right and true for your life. When you have a problem to deal with or a decision to make, pray for guidance, then search the Scriptures, for in them you have light for your path.

Looking again at Isaiah 8:20 above, whoever may be teaching, if they do not speak according to this Word, why should we <u>not</u> listen to them? _____

To be without light (or true enlightenment) means to be without the truth; if the teacher is speaking contrary to the Word of God, they cannot be trusted for spiritual matters or for guidance for your life. The New Covenant reiterates the same revelation about the full authority and sufficiency of God's Word.

> *All Scripture is inspired by God and is useful for teaching, for reproof, for correction, and for training in righteousness (2 Timothy 3:16).*

According to 2 Timothy 3:16, how much of Scripture is inspired?

_____

That's correct, every word of it. "Inspired" literally means "God-breathed." In Genesis 2:7, God's breath gave Adam life. So also, inspired or God-breathed Scripture is God's 'life-giving' Word to you (1 Peter 1:23). This even includes Scriptures that we may not fully understand or enjoy yet! They are still useful for our spiritual growth in our relationship with God. Even as 'veggies' may not be fully appreciated by a child, they are still essential for him or her.

As 1 Peter 2:2 teaches, "As newborn babies, desire the pure milk of the Word, that you may grow thereby." New believers are like babies in the faith. As babies desire milk, so your desire should be for God's Word, the pure milk, which nourishes us spiritually and helps us to grow in the truth. As with babies, regular feeding as well as nourishing meals are vitally important. As Messiah taught us to pray, "give us day by day our daily bread" (Luke 11:3), so we need to have daily meal times in the Word. Can you imagine a baby eating once a week? God's Word is the bread of life for our souls. We need to regularly read and personalize Scripture, praying and seeking to apply God's word to our daily life. This is the way a "baby believer" grows to be mature in the Lord.

Please personalize these verses. Add "me", "my", or "I" for them, they, their, us or our.

"Every word of God is pure; He is a shield to _____ when _____ put _____ trust in Him" (Proverbs 30:5).

"Give _____ day by day _____ daily bread" (Luke 11:3)

For further reading regarding the Bible, see Psalm 19; Psalm 119; Amos 8:11-13; 1 Peter 1:23-25; 2 Peter 1:20, 21; 3:15-16; Revelation 1:3; 22:18-19. For your next appointment, please memorize ("hide in your heart"):

2 Timothy 3:16 –

Isaiah 8:20 –

Also, please memorize the order of the books of the Bible (see Appendix A). It is not very difficult and will greatly facilitate your Bible study time.

Please begin to take at least ten minutes every day to read the Scriptures. Over the next few weeks, after you're reading 10 minutes a day, increase to 20 minutes a day . This, along with your time for prayer, will help you to grow greatly in the grace and knowledge of the Lord. Each day you need to take in the spiritual nourishment of God's Word.

At what time each day, when you're not exhausted or distracted, can you set aside 15 minutes to talk to God (5 minutes of prayer) and hear from God (10 minutes of reading Scripture)? If need be, split the time and read in the morning and pray at night.

_____ *One time period*

_____ *AM time*

_____*PM time*

Let's get started!

Lesson 5

Fellowship

Fellowship means participating with other believers in Yeshua through group worship, the study of the Word, and witnessing to others. This was always an expectation of the Scriptures:

Behold, how good and pleasant it is for brethren to dwell together in unity (Psalm 133:1).

And again-

I was glad when they said to me, "Let us go into the house of the LORD" (Psalm 122:1).

Being in fellowship should be a joy for all children of God. Fellowship is the means that God uses to develop us in His love. Consider the following New Covenant portion:

Speaking the truth in love, we may grow up in all things into Him who is the head, Messiah: from whom the whole body, joined and knit together by what every joint supplies, according to the effective working by which every part does its share, causes growth of the body for the edifying of itself in love (Ephesians 4:15-16).

When you trusted Yeshua as Messiah and Lord, He came to live in you through the Holy Spirit, and by that same Holy Spirit, you were made part of the spiritual body of Messiah (1 Cor. 12:13).

"Body of Messiah" refers to the eternal and spiritual relationship you now have with every other believer in Yeshua. Messiah is the "head of the body" and believers are the various "members of the body." Therefore, our fellowship with one another is the expression and experience of functioning as a body under the direction of Messiah, "the head."

In the body, I may be merely a pinkie, but even so, I have a useful purpose and service for the head. I can scratch, point, and hold things. But this can only occur if I am attached to the body and under the direction of the head. Just like cautions on train tickets (not valid if detached), I am unable to function spiritually when I am not attached to the body. Apart from the body, a severed pinkie, by its erratic movements, may appear to live for a while, but it does so without a useful purpose. A believer who attempts to live without proper fellowship is also useless. He or she may appear alive, but eventually they lose vitality and spiritually wither away.

According to Ephesians 4:15-16, what and how are we to speak to each other?

"the _____ in _____."

We are to be honest and truthful with each other, but not intentionally hurt one another's feelings. Rather, we are to have loving concern for one another. Speaking the truth in love brings about a certain desired result: we spiritually grow together.

According to this same passage, Who do we grow up into? _____

_____

We *grow up in all things into Him, Who is the head of the body, Messiah.* As we mature spiritually, His character is revealed through our individual personalities.

How is the body joined and knit together?

"...by what _____ _____ _____."

Every joint (or member) of the body is important. Each believer is a member that supplies what other members need by "speaking the truth in love," seen in encouragement, affirmation, instruction, and so on. Without fellowship you can neither supply nor be supplied with what we all need for growth.

According to Ephesians 4:15-16 again, what specifically causes growth to the body?

"...according to the _____ _____ by which every part does ____ _____."

"The effective working" refers to the function of a discipled believer. "Its share" refers to every part pitching in and helping the body inside and outside of the congregation.

Finally, what is the result of our growth?

"...for the edifying of itself ___ _____."

Love is one of the chief attributes of our Lord (1 John 4:8). As we spiritually mature to be more like Messiah, we grow in His character. This is one reason why your fellowship with other believers is so vitally important, for your spiritual growth in God's love relationship with you.

Please read Ephesians 4:15-16 in the following <u>personalized</u> format:

> Speaking the truth in love, I and the rest of the fellowship grow up in all things into Him who is the head, Messiah, from whom the whole body, joined and knit together by what I supply and what is supplied to me by my fellow believers, according to our effective working by which I do my share and they do theirs, causes our growth in the body for our building up in love.

Right now, you may not be sure what you supply (your specific purpose or spiritual abilities), but as you grow and mature in fellowship your particular spiritual abilities (or gifts) will develop in loving effectiveness. When you trusted in Messiah and were made part of His spiritual body, you were at that time enabled by the Spirit of God to function as a member of the body.

As you spiritually mature, this enablement will become more evident and relevant. For now, what is most important is to be regularly active in a fellowship that worships the Lord, studies and applies the Scriptures, and demonstrates love one for another even as it exalts Messiah Yeshua.

Please read the following verse:

And let us consider how to provoke [stimulate] one another to love and good deeds, not neglecting the assembling of ourselves together, as is the habit of some, but encouraging one another, and all the more as you see the Day approaching (Hebrews 10:24–25).

In Hebrews 10:24-25 what are you asked to consider?

_____

_____

Since love refers to our attitude toward each other, and good deeds refer to our actions toward each other, why would Hebrews 10:24-25 encourage us to consider both areas in our relationship with one another?

_____

_____.

Please notice the relationship between the exhortation to consider one another and not neglect the assembling of ourselves together. Scripture encourages us to meet together because the Biblical expectation is that we will do so. The purpose is to help each other to spiritually grow in love and good deeds.

Hebrews 10:24-25 acknowledges that some have poor fellowship habits because they are neglecting the assembling of themselves together. Look again at Psalm 122:1, *"I was glad when they said to me, 'Let us go into the house of the LORD'"* and also Psalm 133:1 which speaks of our fellowship as good and pleasant. *"Behold, how good and pleasant it is for brethren to dwell together in unity" (Psalm 133:1).* What is one way you can encourage others in fellowship, and one way others can encourage you?

_____

_____

_____

For further reading there are many portions in the Scriptures that pertain to the subject of fellowship. This would include the books of 1 Corinthians, Ephesians, Philippians, and 1 John, as well as sections such as Genesis 4, 45; Deuteronomy 16:9-12; 2 Samuel 9; Psalm 122, 133; Zechariah 7:8-14, 8:16,17; John 13, 15, 17; Acts 2:41-47; Romans 12, 14, 15:14; Colossians 3; 1 Thessalonians 4; and much of James and 1 Peter.

An interesting study regarding fellowship is also the "one another" sections of the Bible. Besides what is found in the references above you can also refer to: Leviticus 19:11, 25:14-46; Esther 9:19,22; Malachi 3:16; Mark 9:50; Galatians 5:13; 2 Thessalonians 1:3; Titus 3:3; Hebrews 3:13.

Please memorize:

Psalm 133:1 –

Hebrews 10:24-25 –

Please write down where you meet for fellowship, and where it is located:

_____

Now, write down how the Lord ministered in and through you this week at fellowship:

_____

_____

_____

_____

_____

_____

_____

_____

_____

_____

"A new commandment I give to you, that you love one another; as I have loved you, that you also love one another.

"By this all will know that you are My disciples, if you have love for one another." (John 13:34–35)

Lesson 6

Sharing

Sharing your faith is the final relational habit for spiritual growth that we will consider. Prayer and reading Scripture are called "vertical," because they address one's relationship with God. Prayer is you talking to God. Scripture is God talking to you.

Fellowship with other believers and sharing one's faith may be called "horizontal." Fellowship is you relating to people within the body of Messiah. Sharing your faith is you relating to people outside the body of Messiah.

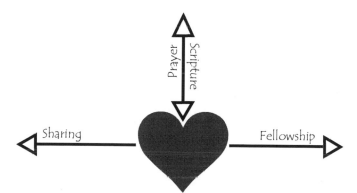

In a sense, you are like a starving person who has found the Bread of Life (John 6:35). Now that your soul is fed and filled, you go and tell others who are starving about this bread that they might live as well. The Scriptures teach that the redeemed share their faith in the Lord with others. Psalm 107:2 says: *"Let the redeemed of the LORD say so!"* And we read in Psalm 96:2-3:

Tell of His salvation from day to day. Declare His glory among the nations, His marvelous works among all the peoples.

God desires to have people trust in Him and be saved:

"Turn to me and be saved, all the ends of the earth! For I am God, and there is no other" (Isaiah 45:22).

He expects His redeemed people to share the truth of who He is, as it says in Isaiah 43:10, *"You are My witnesses,' says the LORD."*

These witnesses had the spiritual responsibility to warn others of their need to turn to the Lord.

> *"If I [the Lord] say to the wicked, 'You shall surely die,' and you give them no warning, or speak to warn the wicked from their wicked way, in order to save their life, those wicked persons shall die for their iniquity; but their blood I will require at your hand. But if you warn the wicked, and they do not turn from their wickedness, or from their wicked way, they shall die for their iniquity; but you will have saved your life" (Ezekiel 3:18-19).*

One example of a reluctant witness was the prophet Jonah. Rather than obey God, Jonah ended up going "not by sail, but by whale." Thus he was a picture of Israel sent by God to warn sinners of God's righteous judgment on sins. Like Jonah, our people have not always been willing to share their faith. However, believers in Yeshua have the same God-given responsibility to tell others the Good News. Yeshua said:

> *"Whoever will confess Me before men, I will also confess that person before My Father who is in heaven. But whoever will deny Me before men, I will also deny that person before My Father who is in heaven" (Matthew 10:32-33).*

Just as you would expect your spouse or even a good friend to introduce you to their acquaintances and not to be ashamed of you, so also Messiah expects those who have trusted in Him to acknowledge Him, and not to be ashamed of Him.

Since you are being discipled, you have obviously already confessed Him to somebody. Again, *mazel tov*: you're off to a great start!

Fortunately, God does not give believers a responsibility without first giving them the power to fulfill it. The New Covenant teaches that all believers are enabled by the Holy Spirit to share their faith as His witnesses:

"But you will receive power when the Holy Spirit has come upon you; and you will be My witnesses in Jerusalem, in all Judea and Samaria, and to the ends of the earth" (Acts 1:8).

We will consider the Holy Spirit in more detail in Lessons 11 and 12, but please notice from this verse that God's power for your life is available for you to be Messiah's witness. The Spirit's power enables you to love the unlovable and live in a way that pleases the Lord, and your new life in Messiah thus demonstrates a life changed by grace. Also, being a witness is who you *are*, not merely something you *do*. If a woman "witnesses" a crime, that person *is* a witness whether or not she speaks up. So also, you are His witness - it is your identity.

There are many new believers that feel very awkward or even frightened to share their faith, especially with their family and friends. But let me share a spiritual secret:

> *The more you give away your faith,*
> *the more faith you have.*

So also, the less you share or give away your faith, the less you have. As you grow in your relationship with the Lord, witnessing to others the truth of Messiah helps you gain spiritual power and mature in the faith. There are various ways to be a witness, confess, or share your faith. Let's consider four of them.

1. The Practical Witness

In Matthew 5:15-16, Messiah taught us to be practical.

> *"Nor do they light a lamp and put it under a basket, but on a lampstand, and it gives light to all who are in the house. Let your light so shine before people, that they may see your good works and glorify your Father in heaven."*

To whom does the lamp (or *menorah*) give light?

"To all who are ____ _____ _____."

This speaks of a house testimony, how we are to live in order to earn the right to be heard. Your family knows you well and usually won't appreciate being "preached" at without seeing a changed life. Please notice carefully what light refers to in Matthew 5:15-16.

It refers to "_____ _____".

God gives believers power, so that His light might be seen in our good works. Many times, these good works are the everyday things that perhaps were neglected or griped about before we trusted in Yeshua: being helpful around the house; taking time to encourage others; excelling at one's job without recognition; having a forgiving attitude; and so on.

According to Matthew 5:15-16 how will people respond when they see your good works?

_____ _____ _____ ___ _____ in heaven.

Not only does a practical witness earn the right to be heard, but it brings glory to our Heavenly Father. Goodness and kindness are the evidence of a changed life, a witness all believers are expected and enabled to have. Acts of kindness (*gemilut chasidim*), both small and large, can open doors to further sharing one's faith with those who see the difference Messiah makes.

2. The Personal/Private Witness

Think of a close friend with whom you can share important personal matters. What can be more important than the Great News of Messiah?

> *Philip found Nathaniel and said to him, "We have found Him of whom Moses in the Law and also the Prophets wrote—Yeshua of Nazareth" (John 1:45).*

Here we see how Philip finds his friend Nathaniel and shares his faith in Yeshua. Notice how Philip refers to Yeshua. He recognized the Messiah through the Torah's words. In fact, there are many prophecies about Yeshua written in the *Torah, Nevi'im* (Prophets), and *Ketuvim* (Writings). Please take the time to read and familiarize yourself with some of these prophecies (see Appendix B). Not only direct predictions, but in fact all Scripture points to Messiah. Even the Biblical feasts have renewed significance in Him. Using Philip as an example, can you think of one friend with whom you can share the wonderful news of Yeshua?

———————————————————————————

Here are a few things you can do to reach out to friends:

- After praying about it, write a letter, or write down what you would want to say to your friend about what has happened in your life. (Acts 1:8; Mark 13)

- Ask the person discipling you to pray with you and possibly come with you to visit your friend.

- Invite your friend to congregational services.

When you do share your faith, remember that you are planting a seed, not an entire tree! Growth is dependent on the Lord, and the results are up to Him. What matters is to be faithful.

> *I [Paul] planted the seed, Apollos watered it, but God made it grow. (1 Corinthians 3:6)*

Here are some great words to follow on the point:

> *Conduct yourselves wisely toward outsiders, making the most of the time. Let your speech always be gracious, seasoned with salt, so that you may know how you ought to answer everyone (Colossians 4:5-6).*

"Seasoned with salt" is like giving tidbits, not the whole meal at once. A little salt makes food tasty; whereas salty food is hard to stomach. The idea is to share a bit at a time so you can gauge your friend's interest. When you see your friend become disinterested, it is time to stop for a while. If you see some responsiveness, you can share a little more. What a joy it is to share the Lord and see friends become brothers and sisters in Messiah!

3. The Proclaiming/Public Witness

There are times when the Lord provides opportunity for believers to publicly proclaim their faith. These opportunities are usually reserved for the experienced, trained and mature in the faith. I say "usually" because you never know what the Lord may have for you.

> *[Yeshua] said to them, "Thus it is written, that the Messiah is to suffer and to rise from the dead on the third day, and that repentance and forgiveness of sins is to be proclaimed in His Name to all nations, beginning from Jerusalem. You are witnesses of these things" (Luke 24:46–48).*

What is to be proclaimed?

"_____ and _____ of _____ is to be proclaimed in His Name."

A public witness can begin with sharing in your home congregation how you came to faith in Yeshua. Or, with others from your congregation, you might hand out Good News literature to passersby in a shopping, business, or recreation area. Sometimes, a public witness may be sharing Messiah's hope and love at a hospital or homeless shelter. Or, as we see below in Luke 12, it may even be in front of the courts. In any case, we are to trust in Yeshua each time to give us the words to speak. He has promised He will do just that!

> *"When you are brought before synagogues, rulers and authorities, do not worry about how you will defend yourselves or what you will say, for the Holy Spirit will teach you at that time what you should say" (Luke 12:11–12).*

Ask God to prepare you for just the right opportunity. You can make your faith practical by writing down your story or "testimony" (about five minutes in length) of how you came to faith in Yeshua. Here's one format for sharing if you have the opportunity:

- The first minute or so speak about your life before Messiah: some of your background and areas of recognized spiritual need.

- The second minute or so speak about how you came to trust in Messiah; what issues of Yeshua were most meaningful and attractive to you.

- The third minute and concluding minutes, speak about your life since you trusted in Yeshua: answers to prayer; changes in your life; peace in your heart; perhaps ending with a Scripture verse that is meaningful to you.

Once you have written down your testimony, share with the person discipling you at your next scheduled appointment. A public witness can be a joyous victory in the Lord!

4. The Persuasive Witness

Though you need never be a *pushy* witness, you can be a *persuasive* witness. To persuade is to urge someone to action, or convince by appealing to reason and understanding. Consider this Scripture:

> *We must all appear before the judgment seat of Messiah, so that each one may be recompensed for his deeds in the body, according to what he has done, whether good or bad. Therefore, knowing the fear of the Lord, we persuade others (2 Corinthians 5:10-11).*

What motivates a persuasive witness?

"knowing ____ _____ ____ _____ _____."

"The fear of the Lord" is tied to "the judgment seat of Messiah." Thus, the reality of judgment upon the lost compels us to share. As it is developed through study and practice, a believer can be a very persuasive and bold servant of God (like Stephen, Acts 6:8-10; or Apollos, Acts 18:24-28). Sometimes this persuasiveness is a particular gift God has given you at salvation or during a time of opportunity.

> *But one and the same Spirit works all these things, distributing to each one individually as He wills (1 Corinthians 12:11).*

The Biblical truths studied in the next section will serve to further build you up in this matter. No matter how much you know, it is crucial to remain humble, recognizing when you do not know the answers to questions. This particular gift is not given to every believer, but all are encouraged to consider the deeper issues of the faith and to *"always be ready to give an answer for the hope that is within you" (1 Peter 3:15).*

Please memorize these Scriptures for the next appointment:

Psalm 96:3 –

Matthew 5:15–16 –

This week, pray that God will have someone with whom you can share your faith. Then be ready to share!

Take a moment to reflect on the insights and spiritual disciplines (prayer, Scripture study, fellowship and sharing your faith) that God is incorporating into your life.

PART 3

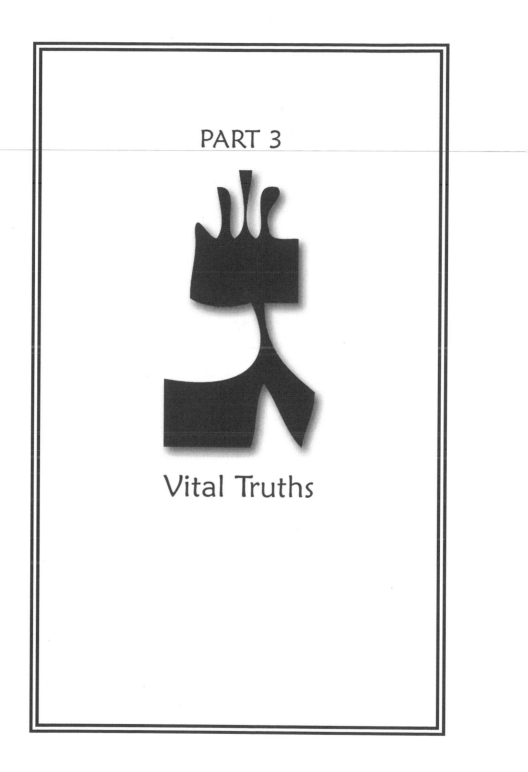

Vital Truths

Lesson 7

The Scriptures and "the Oral Law"

Deepening your spiritual roots includes understanding why the present majority of the Jewish people do not accept the truth of God's Word regarding your faith in Yeshua. Just as sharing Messiah has benefits for your own spiritual walk, so also these are truths for your edification.

The Scriptures tell us to expect that only a remnant would accept God's salvation, whether it be in the days of Elijah the Prophet, or the days of Isaiah, or at the present time (1 Kings 19:18; Isaiah 10:21; Romans 11:5). Yet, many believers have a concern to understand some of the traditional objections to faith in Yeshua, so as to be able to share Messiah. It is to these vital truths we now turn.

The objections of the next three chapters all deal with the Word of God. By "the Word of God," we are referring to two aspects of God's revelation of Himself: the Scriptures, and Messiah. Both are described as the Word of God.

- The Scripture of God is His Word Inscribed, or written down. This is the special revelation of God that proclaims the only way of salvation.

- The Son of God is His Word Incarnate ("in the flesh," John 1:1, 14; Hebrews 1:1-3). He is the redemption of God Who alone provides the way of salvation.

The Scripture of God and the Son of God perfectly reveal God's character and concern for you. Tragically, Rabbinic Judaism has rejected both what the Scriptures proclaim, and what the Son provides regarding our salvation.

Both Jewish and Gentile believers should comprehend these differences surrounding this split, seeking to be a bridge. These issues are presented so that as you study and appreciate the Scriptural basis of these vital truths, your faith will be strengthened, your spiritual roots will be deepened, and you will have even more confidence in Messiah Yeshua!

What is Our Foundation?

An Orthodox Jewish man was asked by a believing Jewish acquaintance to read Isaiah 53 and decide what it teaches. The Orthodox man responded, "I will decide what it teaches after I first study what the traditional interpretation is in the Oral Law." In Orthodox Judaism, one should not attempt to understand the Scriptures apart from the traditional explanation as laid out in the Oral Law. To the Orthodox Jew, the Oral Law is the authoritative interpretation of the Scriptures.

Oral Law refers to the Talmud, which is a compilation of Rabbinic commentaries on the first five books of Moses, called the Torah. The Talmud, completed around 500 CE, consists of the Mishnah as well as commentary on the Mishnah called Gemara (Mishnah + Gemara = Talmud). The tradition grew to include a further compendium called Midrash until about the 12th century (these terms can be found in the glossary in the back).

Sadly, when Christendom had power it often persecuted the Jewish people with ferocity; this even extended to mass burnings of the Talmud. This sort of evil has deep roots and is addressed in two of our books, *Even You Can Share the Jewish Messiah*, and *The Messianic Answer Book*. For now let us note that the Talmud contains much beauty, wisdom, and valuable historical information. It should go without saying perhaps, but any approach which seeks to destroy literature or force people to believe is contrary to the approach of Messiah. Regardless, the basic issue we need to consider is whether this tradition should have *ultimate authority*. Indeed, it should not.

The authority granted the Oral Law is based on a theory about its origin. The Talmud itself claims that along with the Law from God at Mount Sinai that was written down, Moses also received revelation from God which was *not* originally written down, but "transmitted" orally—thus, the Oral Law. This claim to authority is found in the following well known quotation from the Talmud:

"Moses received the Torah at Sinai and transmitted it to Joshua, Joshua to the Elders, and the Elders to the Prophets, and the Prophets to the men of the Great Synagogue" (Pirke Avot 1a).

Rabbi J. Israelstam explains the meaning of this passage: "the transmission and reception were done orally through a continuous succession of 'schools' headed by the Elders, prophets and scribes of their respective generations." In other words, the claim is that there was revelation from God separate to the Scriptures and passed down alongside the written Word.

This tradition was allegedly transmitted orally to keep the proper interpretation of Scripture out of Gentile hands, until it eventually had to be written down or perish (Avi Shafran, *JewThink*, p. 26-28). As plausible as this may or may not appear, the origin comes into question. If the Talmud's claim to originate as Oral Law is untrue - that is, if the Oral Law was not given by God to Moses - then it is an unreliable tradition, and not to be given divine authority.

The written Scriptures speak directly to this issue. First, we need to recognize the basic and authoritative assumption of the Bible as a whole.

Notice 2 Timothy 3:16, *"All Scripture is inspired by God."* The word used for Scripture in the Greek is *graphe*. This is the Greek word for "writing," similar to the Hebrew usage of *ketav* as in Daniel 10:21, "But I will tell you what is noted in the *Scripture* of truth." The word "Scripture" simply, but quite importantly, means "Writings."

The point the Bible makes is that whatever "truth" was authoritatively inspired by God was written down. This fact directly contradicts the rabbinical idea and traditional premise for the origin and authority of the Oral Law.

But beyond this, the Scriptures directly teach the impossibility of an Oral Law from Moses on Mount Sinai, or anywhere else.

To understand this we should look at Exodus 24, which describes Moses' return to the people of Israel after receiving the Law from God on Mount Sinai:

So Moses came and told the people all the words of the LORD and all the ordinances. And all the people answered with one voice and said, "All the words which the LORD has said we will do."

And Moses wrote down all the words of the LORD...

Then he took the Book of the Covenant and read it in the hearing of the people. And they said, "All that the LORD has said we will do, and be obedient." (Exodus 24:3-4, 7)

In Exodus 24:3, how many words of the Lord did Moses tell the people? "_____."

So Moses shared <u>all</u> of God's words to him. The Hebrew word *kol* means "all": there was nothing else to share.

In Exodus 24:4, how many words of the Lord did Moses write down? "_____."

So Moses wrote down all (*kol*, again) the words of the Lord. There was nothing else left over to "transmit" orally; no leftover Torah, no Oral Law!

In Exodus 24:7, when Moses read to the people from the Book of the Covenant the same words of the Lord that he had shared with them earlier (24:3), the words were recognized as the same and complete words they had heard by responding in the same manner. *"All that the LORD has said we will do."* There simply was no Oral Law from Moses at Mount Sinai.

But some may ask, is it not possible that perhaps a day, a month, a year, or a decade or two later, Moses remembered further revelation from God on Mount Sinai, and then transmitted it orally? Did Moses wake up one morning and say, "Wow! I just remembered all kinds of neat laws God had told me. Let's just keep it an Oral Law for the next 1600 years, OK?" No, it is not at all possible.

Though the Talmud, in the section above from Pirke Avot, states that Moses "transmitted it to Joshua," the Scriptures actually state otherwise. We read in Joshua 1:8:

> *"This Book of the Law shall not depart out of your mouth; you shall meditate on it day and night, so that you may be careful to act in accordance with all that is <u>written</u> in it. For then you shall make your way prosperous, and then you shall be successful."*

There was no Oral Law from Moses on Mount Sinai transmitted to Joshua. It was all written (*katuv*). Yet notice the beautiful promise for success found in that verse—based not upon keeping the Oral Law, but upon what was written.

According to Joshua 1:8, what are we to do with the Scriptures "day and night?"

"You shall _____ on it day and night".

Meditate, *hagah*, means to "think over deeply" about the Scriptures. It is like chewing your food well in order to obtain all the nutrients. Even as it is used similarly in Psalm 1:2—*"But his delight is in the law of the LORD, and in His law he meditates day and night."*

According to Joshua 1:8, why should you meditate on the Scriptures?

"So that you may be careful to _____ ___ _____ with all that is <u>written</u> in it."

The most fulfilling way to live life is to act in accordance with all that is written in the Scriptures. Why?

According to Joshua 1:8, what happens when you act in accordance with the written Scriptures?

"For then you shall make your way _____, and then you shall be _____."

Being spiritually prosperous and spiritually successful results from following the spiritual truths of God's Word, the written Word. These two words characterize the fruits of the Spirit, or the spiritual character of God as listed in Galatians 5:22-23. Being spiritually prosperous and successful is having God's character (called having a "godly" character) as you live for God by living out His written Word that you have hidden in your heart (Psalm 119:11). Personalize Joshua 1:8:

> "This Book of the Law shall not depart out of ____ mouth; ____ shall meditate on it day and night, so that ____ may be careful to act in accordance with all that is <u>written</u> in it. For then ____ shall make ____ way prosperous, and then ____ shall be successful."

Though this verse contains a wonderful promise, it is also clear that Joshua knew nothing about following an Oral Law, but only about acting in accordance with the written Word of God.

Four hundred years later, at the end of King David's life and at the beginning of Solomon's reign, the written Scriptures again state plainly that there was still only the written Law of Moses. Read and note this in the following portion from 1 Kings 2:3:

> *"And keep the charge of the LORD your God, walking in his ways and keeping His statutes, His commandments, His ordinances, and His testimonies, as it is <u>written</u> in the Law of Moses, so that you may prosper in all that you do and wherever you turn."*

As with Joshua, David affirmed the authority of the Written Word four centuries later. Even at that time, there simply was no Oral Law from Moses at Mount Sinai. Throughout the Older Covenant and even in the Prophets, there is no Oral Law, only the Written Law from Moses (for further study, consider Joshua 8:31-32; 23:6; 2 Kings 14:6; 23:25; 1 Chronicles 16:40; 2 Chronicles 23:18; 25:4; 30:16; 31:3; 35:26; Ezra 3:2; 7:6; Nehemiah 8:1,14; 10:34-36; Daniel 9:11-13; Malachi 4:4).

Nothing Compares to God's Word

The Hebrew Scriptures make it clear: there was not then, nor is there today, any Oral Law from Moses. The Oral Law are traditions of men, and should not be compared in authority to the written Word of God.

God revealed the truth authoritatively and permanently to His people—yes, even you—by having it written down. The New Covenant relies upon this same principle as well, as these next few examples demonstrate.

> *And truly Yeshua did many other signs in the presence of His disciples, which are not <u>written</u> in this book; but these are <u>written</u> that you may believe that Yeshua is the Messiah, the Son of God, and that believing you may have life in His name (John 20:30-31).*

> *And consider that the longsuffering of our Lord is salvation—as also our beloved brother Paul, according to the wisdom given to him, has <u>written</u> to you, as also in all his letters, speaking in them of these things, in which are some things hard to understand, which untaught and unstable people twist to their own destruction, as they do also <u>the rest of the Scriptures</u> (2 Peter 3:15-16).*

> *Blessed is he who reads and those who hear the words of this prophecy, and keep those things that are <u>written</u> in it; for the time is near (Revelation 1:3).*

> *For I testify to everyone who hears the words of the prophecy of this <u>book</u>: If anyone adds to these things, God will add to him the plagues that are <u>written</u> in this book; and if anyone takes away from the words of the book of this prophecy, God shall take away his part from the Book of Life, from the holy city, and from the things which are <u>written</u> in this book (Revelation 22:18-19).*

All this is stated in order to make some simple applications for your life. If someone claiming rabbinic authority states that your faith in Yeshua is not proper or not Jewish because of what is traditionally believed from the Oral Law, you need not give such words any credence. The written Word of God (both Old and New Covenants) proves the validity of your faith in Yeshua.

Also, if even a "New Covenant believer in Yeshua" approaches you and wants to give you a personal "revelation from God," give it no credence either. It may seem encouraging, but it is not authoritative. The written Scriptures, both Old and New Covenants, are God's only authoritative truth for your life.

The Corinthian believers were desirous of "mystical experiences." Therefore, Paul warned in 1 Corinthians 4:6 *"that you may learn in us not to go beyond __what is written__."* Stick to the written Word of God for all faith and practice.

Try personalizing this same portion from 1 Corinthians 4:6:

> "...that ___ may learn (from the Apostles) not to go beyond what is written."

Every eternal truth of God for our lives and redemption is fully contained in the very Bible you study. What confidence all believers can have knowing that *"All Scripture is inspired by God and is useful..."* *(2 Timothy 3:16)*. Please review this verse and 1 John 5:13, and memorize Joshua 1:8. Remember you are to do what the Scripture teaches.

May you continue to grow in spiritual confidence and maturity, as you trust and follow the truth of God's inscribed Word!

As newborn babes,
desire the pure milk of the Word,
that you may grow thereby
(1 Peter 2:2).

Lesson 8

The Divine Messiah

There are two basic facts the Scriptures declare regarding the nature of Messiah that are necessary to genuine faith in the one, true God:

1. Yeshua is God. Yeshua is declared to be *Adonai* (Lord), the Son of God, and in fact, God incarnate. The present chapter deals with this matter and it will lead to the further consideration of the "Trinity" (Lesson 10).

2. Yeshua is Good. Since Yeshua is Lord, He is by definition without sin: if He had sinned, He would not be God, for God cannot sin. If He had sinned, Yeshua would need atonement and forgiveness, and could not be the sinless sacrifice necessary for remission of our sins (Lesson 9).

These two issues are where those who believe in Rabbinic Judaism differ with all Messianic Jews and Biblical Judaism. Since Rabbinic Judaism denies the deity of Yeshua and the suffering of Messiah, we will consider these issues.

Traditional Judaism rejects the possibility for Yeshua to have been God come in the flesh. This view is represented in Maimonides' Thirteen Principles of Faith, written in the Middle Ages. These principles are also called the *Ani Ma'amin* (Hebrew for "I believe"), since each article of faith begins with the phrase "I believe with perfect faith." They were seemingly written in reaction to a dominant and often hostile European Christendom.

The third principle reads:

> *I believe with perfect faith that the Creator, blessed be His name, is not a body, and that He is free from all the accidents of matter, and that He has not any form whatsoever.*

In the traditional interpretation, this is taken to mean that God cannot come in the flesh. But is that true? While it is true that God "is not a body" —God's essence is Spirit—is it really impossible for God to come in human flesh? The Scriptures teach us never to underestimate the Lord, *"for with God nothing shall be impossible!"* (Luke 1:37; Genesis 18:14). What the Hebrew Scriptures prophesied and the New Covenant declares is that in Yeshua, the God of Israel came in the flesh.

Three basic questions are normally raised on this issue, which help us consider it more fully.

1. Can God Come in the Flesh?

To find the answer, we will visit Abraham in Genesis 18 where the text states in verse one that *"God appeared to Abraham by the Oaks of Mamre."* In the next verse it states that *"as he lifted his eyes, three men stood by him."* Abraham and Sarah then prepared food for these *"guests" (18:3-8).* Was it merely a vision? Impossible, for not only do people not prepare food for a vision, but also, visions don't eat! These "men" did (*"...and they ate," 18:8*).

Now, two of these three "men" are later identified as angels (compare Genesis 18:22 and 19:1). But the third one that *noshed, shmoozed* and *shlepped* with Abraham ("ate," "spoke," and "walked," verses 8, 10, 16, 22) is identified as the Lord Himself.

> *And the LORD said to Abraham, "Why did Sarah laugh, saying, 'Shall I surely bear a child, since I am old?' Is anything too hard for the LORD? At the appointed time I will return to you, according to the time of life, and Sarah shall have a son" (Genesis 18:13-14).*

We see the Lord God asking a rhetorical question, *"Is anything too hard for the LORD?"* What is the implied answer?

_____!

That's right, nothing is too hard for the Lord. Your problems may be too much for you to handle, but they are not too much for God to handle. This is why you can cast all your anxieties upon Him. In Yeshua, you can do all things through Messiah who strengthens you (Philippians 4:13). In fact, this is a major theme of Scripture:

55

God is able (For further study, see Matthew 3:9; Luke 3:8; Romans 11:23; 14:4; 2 Corinthians 9:8; Hebrews 11:19)!

In Genesis 18:13, the text states *"And the LORD said to Abraham..."* The word translated LORD throughout this portion is sometimes called the *Tetragrammaton*. It is the four Hebrew letters that make up the sacred Name of God: י *yud*, ה *hey*, ו *vav*, ה *hey* (pronounced by some as *Yahweh*, or *Jehovah*). The LORD God Himself came, visited, *noshed* and *shmoozed*, then left after His talk with His friend Abraham.

Do the Hebrew Scriptures teach that God can, and in fact, did come in the flesh? Clearly the answer is yes! God is not only able to enter into this time-space continuum, but He did so. And the Scriptures are the authority on God manifesting Himself (Exodus 24:10; Joshua 5:13-6:2).

2. But Biblically, was Messiah Expected to be God Incarnate?

This question may be understood as saying, "Okay, maybe God can do anything, but does that necessarily mean that a human Messiah was to be God?" In fact, the prophets, especially Isaiah and Micah, most directly answer this:

> *For a child shall be born to us and a son shall be given; and the government shall be upon His shoulder; and His name shall be called: Wonderful Counselor, Mighty God, Everlasting Father, Prince of Peace (Isaiah 9:6[5])."*

This portion is traditionally recognized as referring to the Messiah:

> *I have yet to raise up the Messiah, of whom it is written, "for a child is born to us (Isaiah 9:5)" (Midrash Deuteronomy Rabbah 1.20, emphasis mine).*

In this section Isaiah predicts that One coming:

✡ from the *"Galilee" (9:1)*

✡ will bring *"light," "joy," (9:2-3)*

✡ and *"victorious peace" (9:4-5)*

✡ for He is the *"Prince of Peace" (Sar Shalom, 9:6).*

✡ Thus, He is also called the *"Mighty God" (El Gibbor, 9:6).*

This *"child to be born"* is the theme of Isaiah 7-11, where it states He would be:

✡ *"born of a virgin" (7:14)*

✡ *"the Root of Jesse...to whom the Gentiles will seek" (11:10)*

✡ sought by *"the remnant of Israel" (10:20-23).*

That last point verifies the fact that *not* every Jewish person will believe, but only *"the remnant shall return, the remnant of Jacob, to the Mighty God" (El Gibbor again, Isaiah 10:21).*

Micah the prophet gives further detail about Messiah's Divine Nature, and also specifically states *where* He would be born.

> *But you, Bethlehem Ephratah, little among the thousands of Judah, out of you will go forth for Me, one who will be ruler in Israel, whose goings forth have been from <u>days of eternity</u> (Micah 5:2[1]).*

Micah clearly states that Israel's Ruler would not only be born in Bethlehem, but his goings forth would be from eternity (*mimey olam,* lit.- "days of eternity"). That is, He who would be born in Bethlehem is the Eternal One; God! Before Messiah Yeshua was born—and therefore, before this verse caused any controversy—Micah 5:1 was indisputably recognized by the Rabbinical community as referring to the Eternal Messiah. In the century prior to the birth of Yeshua, the Rabbis used an Aramaic paraphrase called *targum* ("translation"). Here is one such translation:

> *And you, Bethlehem Ephratah, you who were too small to be numbered among the thousands of the house of Judah, from you shall come forth before Me <u>the Messiah</u>, to exercise dominion over Israel,*

he whose name was mentioned <u>from before, from the days of creation</u> (Targum Jonathan to Micah 5:1).

Normative Jewish thinking referred this passage to Messiah, the Eternal One. The Biblical truth is that the Messiah, the One to bring peace, joy and life to all who believe - the same One who would be born in Bethlehem, yet live in Galilee - this One who is the Lord, the Mighty God Himself!

In Appendix B you will find more prophetic Scriptures from *Tanakh* (or Older Covenant) that God would come in the flesh to earth, and that Messiah's nature would be divine.

3. But, does the New Covenant Proclaim Yeshua as Messiah and God?

The word "Christ" is a transliteration, not a translation. It should be translated Messiah ("Anointed One") from the Greek, *christos*. Christ is not Yeshua's last name, but His title, Messiah. Therefore, hundreds of times the New Covenant unequivocally declares Yeshua to be the Messiah.

Similarly Messiah's Deity is declared hundreds of times as well by His title "Lord," and His identification as "the LORD" of the Older Covenant.

> *The beginning of the Gospel of Messiah Yeshua, the Son of God. As it is written in Isaiah the Prophet: "Behold, I send My messenger before Your face, who will prepare Your way before You. The voice of one crying in the wilderness: 'Prepare the way of the LORD; make His paths straight'" (Mark 1:1-3).*

This portion repeats Malachi 3:1 and Isaiah 40:3, *"Prepare the way of the LORD,"* where the personal Name of God is used. The New Covenant writers were clearly identifying Yeshua as the one true God, the God of Israel come in the flesh (Hebrews 1:8-12). New Covenant writers were clear regarding His Divine nature, as much as they were clear regarding His human nature:

In the beginning was the Word, the Word was with God, the Word was God ... and the Word became flesh and dwelt among us (John 1:1, 14).

And in saying this, the New Covenant writers also reported exactly what the Messiah Himself declared:

"I and the Father are one" (John 10:30).

"If you had known Me, you would have known My Father also; and from now on you know Him and have seen Him." Philip said to Him, "Lord, show us the Father, and it is sufficient for us." Yeshua said to him, "Have I been with you so long, and yet you have not known Me, Philip? He who has seen Me has seen the Father; so how can you say, 'Show us the Father'?" (John 14:7-9).

Often, the writers assume rather than explain the Divinity of Yeshua, using it as a standard to make practical application for our lives. This is what we see in Philippians 2:3-8:

Do nothing from selfish ambition or conceit, but in humility regard others as better than yourselves. Let each of you look not to your own interests, but to the interests of others.

Your attitude should be the same as Messiah, Who being in very nature God, did not consider equality with God something to be grasped, but humbled Himself, taking on the form of a servant, coming in human appearance. In that form of a man, He humbled Himself and became obedient unto death, even death by the cross.

What should your attitude be?

My attitude should be ____ _____ __ _____.

If your attitude should be the same as Messiah's, and if Messiah was willing to place your interests before His own, what interests should we look out for?

"Let each of you look not to your own interests, but ____ ___ _____ ___ _____."

Before Messiah humbled Himself, taking on the form of a servant, coming in human appearance, what was always His nature?

"Who being in _____ _____ _____."

Since He was by nature the eternal God, why did He humble Himself?

Because He "did not consider equality _____ ____ _____ __ __ _____."

That is, He did not need to hold on to the position or status of God in order to demonstrate the love and righteousness of God. Coming as man and dying for our sins could perfectly demonstrate that.

If He who is God did nothing from selfish ambition or conceit, but in humility regarded others as better than Himself, what should be your attitude toward others?

"Do nothing from ____ _____ __ _____ ____, but in humility _____ _____ ___ _____ _____ yourselves."

Consider yet a few more New Covenant verses regarding the Messiah's nature as God.

✿ *He is the image of the invisible God (Colossians 1:15).*

✿ *For in Messiah dwells all the fullness of the Godhead bodily; and you are complete in Him, who is the head of all principality and power (Colossians 2:9-10).*

In the original language of that last verse, "fullness" is the same Greek word as "complete." Because He is completely God, you are complete in Him! Personalize this verse by exchanging "you are" with "I am" in Colossians 2:9-10.

"For in Messiah dwells all the fullness of the Godhead bodily; and ___ ____ complete in Him, Who is the head of all principality and power."

Now try just the one phrase in 2:10, "and ____ ____ complete in Him."

Here are some other New Covenant Scriptures declaring Yeshua the Messiah as *Adonai*, or the Lord:

✡ *God, Who at various times and in various ways spoke in time past to the fathers by the prophets, has in these last days spoken to us by His Son, whom He has appointed heir of all things, through whom also He made the worlds; who being the brightness of His glory and the express image of His person, and upholding all things by the word of His power, when He had by Himself purged our sins, sat down at the right hand of the Majesty on high (Hebrews 1:1-3).*

✡ *The revelation of Messiah Yeshua, the Faithful Witness, the Firstborn of the dead, and the Ruler of the kings of the earth. To Him Who loves us and freed us from our sins by His blood, and made us to be a kingdom of priests serving His God and Father, to Him be glory and dominion forever and ever. Amen. Look! He is coming with the clouds; every eye will see Him. "I am the Alpha and the Omega," says the Lord God, "Who is and Who was and Who is to come, the Almighty" (Revelation 1:1, 5-8).*

✡ *And the Lord God of the holy prophets sent His angel to show His servants the things which must shortly take place. "And behold, I am coming quickly, and My reward is with Me, to give to every one according to his work. I am the Alpha and the Omega, the Beginning and the End, the First and the Last. I, Yeshua, have sent My angel to testify to you these things in the churches. I am the Root and the Offspring of David, the Bright and Morning Star" (Revelation 22:6, 12, 13, 16).*

What amazing love is demonstrated in the humility of our Messiah! The One who is the Eternal God, *Adonai*, the First and the Last came in the flesh to die for our sins that we might have forgiveness, life, joy, and peace, by trusting in His atoning sacrifice for our sins.

Some mistakenly think that we believe that a man became God. No man can become God. But God became a man as He incarnated

His life and love through Yeshua, the Messiah of Israel and Savior of the World. Nothing is impossible for God!

Memorize Isaiah 9:6, Micah 5:2, and John 1:1.

How would you answer this question?

"I'm Jewish and I'm impressed with the life of Yeshua, but how can I as a Jew believe he is Adonai/Lord?"

_____

_____

_____

_____

_____

_____

_____

_____

Lesson 9

The Suffering Messiah

Though it is an uncommon opinion today, there are some who consider Yeshua to be a bad person. Why? One reason for this is that so much evil has been perpetrated against the Jewish people in His Name. Those who are unaware of the Jewishness of the New Covenant may assume that Yeshua taught Jew-hatred, since many of His so-called followers seemed to be vicious anti-Semites.

If one does not accept the Scriptures in general, and the New Covenant in particular, as God's inerrant Word, then the issues of virgin birth, miracles and resurrections all seem like a religious rationalization for a hoax played upon ignorant and gullible people.

Besides all this, the authoritative guide for Orthodox Judaism, the Talmud, makes some unfortunate and inaccurate remarks in reference to Yeshua and His earliest followers:

> On the eve of Passover Yeshu was hanged. For forty days before his execution took place, a herald went forth and cried, "He is going forth to be stoned because he has practiced sorcery and enticed Israel to apostasy. Any one who can say anything in his favour, let him come forward and plead on his behalf." But since nothing was brought forward in his favour he was hanged on the eve of Passover!—Ulla retorted "Do you suppose that he was one for whom a defense could be made? Was he not a Mesith (enticer), concerning whom Scripture says, 'Neither shalt thou spare, neither shalt thou conceal him'?" With Yeshu however it was different, for he was connected with the government (or royalty, i.e., influential). Our Rabbis taught: "Yeshu had five disciples, Matthai, Nakai, Nezerm, Buni and Todah" (Sanhedrin 43a).

Why would the Talmud, referring to Him as "Yeshu" (an acrostic meaning *yemach shmo vezichro*, or "may His name be blotted out forever," instead of Yeshua, which means "the Lord saves"), say that He "practiced sorcery and enticed Israel to apostasy"? Likewise, why did they conclude that he was therefore was as an "enticer" (i.e., deceiver)?

This language can seem jarring today, in an age when many desire Yeshua to be merely a good teacher! But understand that since the writers of the Talmud did not believe in or accept Yeshua as Messiah, they had to explain Him away.

For example, they had to deal with the objective evidence of the many people Yeshua had healed in Judea, who were still walking around in the first century when many of the quoted rabbis lived! Therefore, they claimed Yeshua "practiced sorcery," which, incidentally, is the same accusation recorded in Matthew 12:22-29. In doing this, however, the Talmud thereby indirectly testifies to Yeshua's supernatural miracles. The Talmud can only distort this by attributing it to "sorcery."

Also, it is easy to understand why the word "enticer" is used for Yeshua. After all, the Talmudic writers could not deny the great numbers of Jewish people that had come to faith in Yeshua. Dr. Louis Goldberg, professor of Jewish Studies at Moody Bible College, taught that as many as one-third of the Jewish people of the first century had come to faith in Yeshua. While the Talmud is inaccurate in its moral judgment about Yeshua, it testifies to the inexplicable reality of His ancient movement of Jewish and Gentile followers!

Since the 19th century, some have even tried to blame Paul for the creation of faith in Messiah, making Yeshua into merely a good, though misunderstood Jew. In so doing they have to disassociate the *words* of Yeshua from the *Person* of Yeshua. In dismissing much of the Good News record about Yeshua as inaccurate, the skeptics dismiss the Yeshua found in these texts as irrelevant.

The evidence which has come to be accepted in scholarly circles stand squarely against this old-guard skepticism. Ironically, in rediscovering the ancient Jewishness of the Biblical texts, many scholars have come to argue on the evidence for their basic historical validity. In fact, it is the critics and skeptics who are concocting a new Yeshua, in order to make Paul into the bad guy!

But the question will always be raised, "if Jesus is so good, then why did he die on a cross, like a common criminal?"

The Need for Messiah's Atonement

It is true that Yeshua died as a criminal. In order to understand how Yeshua could be good, yet suffer and die in a shameful manner, we will need to consider the backdrop that Tanakh provides to this issue. We already learned from Torah that blood was necessary to atone for the sins of the people (Genesis 3:21; 4:4; Leviticus 16:27; 17:11). Sin was that serious. Yet, the whole sacrificial system - which could only cover sin from year to year - pointed to the Coming One that would provide an everlasting atonement.

> ✿ *I gave My back to those who strike Me, and My cheeks to those who pluck out the beard; I did not cover My face from humiliation and spitting (Isaiah 50:6).*

> ✿ *...after the sixty-two weeks the Messiah will be cut off and have nothing (Daniel 9:26).*

Perhaps the most significant portion predicting Messiah's suffering is Isaiah 53. Here is one section of that portion.

> *53:3 He was despised and forsaken of men, a man of sorrows and acquainted with grief; and like one from whom men hide their face He was despised, and we did not esteem Him.*

> *4 Surely our griefs He Himself bore, and our sorrows He carried; yet we ourselves esteemed Him stricken, smitten of God, and afflicted.*

> *5 But He was pierced through for our transgressions, He was crushed for our iniquities; the chastening for our well being fell upon Him, and by His scourging we are healed.*

> *6 All of us like sheep have gone astray, each of us has turned to his own way; but the LORD has caused the iniquity of us all to fall on Him.*

> *7 He was oppressed and He was afflicted, yet He did not open His mouth; like a lamb that is led to slaughter, and like a sheep that is silent before its shearers, so He did not open His mouth.*

> *8 By oppression and judgment He was taken away; and as for His*

generation, who considered that He was cut off out of the land of the living for the transgression of my people, to whom the stroke was due?

Isaiah wrote this portion (around 700 BCE) both to illustrate the model of God's perfect Servant, and to give Israel hope in the coming Redeemer. The point of this portion is that though Messiah the Servant would suffer terribly, He would be eternally successful. Please note that 52:13-15 teaches that the Messiah would be successful to the degree that he suffered. The portion of 53:1-9 teaches that Messiah would be successful despite His sufferings. In 53:10-12 the Messiah would be successful due to His sufferings:

10 But the LORD was pleased to crush Him, putting Him to grief; if He would render Himself as a guilt offering, He will see His offspring, He will prolong His days, and the good pleasure of the LORD will prosper in His hand.

11 As a result of the anguish of His soul, He will see it and be satisfied; by His knowledge the Righteous One, My Servant, will justify the many, as He will bear their iniquities.

12 Therefore, I will allot Him a portion with the great, and He will divide the spoil with the strong; because He poured out Himself to death, and was numbered with the transgressors; yet He Himself bore the sin of many, and interceded for the transgressors.

Though this portion was traditionally recognized as referring to the Messiah, the obvious clarity to this fact became a problem for traditional Judaism. Believers in Yeshua used Isaiah 53 so often to proclaim Yeshua, that Rashi, the famous 11th century Rabbi, popularized a counter interpretation. Rashi said that Isaiah 53 refers not to Messiah, but to Israel! When many of my people objectively read this portion, however, the response can often be something like, "How did the New Testament get into my side of the Bible?"

The purpose for Messiah's suffering and death was to make atonement. He suffered and died, not merely as a martyr or hero, but to accomplish the atonement for the sins of all who believe in Him.

Isaiah 53 calls this an *asham*, that is, a trespass offering for sin. The New Covenant refers to Messiah's atonement this way:

> *He [God] made Him who knew no sin to be sin on our behalf, so that we might become the righteousness of God in Him (2 Corinthians 5:21).*

The Scriptures agree: Messiah, though innocent of sin, would come to suffer and die for our sins. Therefore, it was necessary for Messiah to suffer innocently and to be wrongly assumed guilty (Isaiah 53:4).

Yeshua is God, and He is Good!

Please memorize Isaiah 53:4-6.

How would you answer this question:

"I am impressed with the life of Jesus, but why did he suffer and die so terribly?" Please write out your answer.

_____

_____

_____

_____

_____

_____

_____

"Behold the Lamb of God, who takes away the sin of the world" (John 1:29).

Lesson 10

The Tri-unity:

God's Unique Unity

There is no one like God. Yet, an infamous misconception about the faith of New Covenant believers is that we teach "belief in three gods." For many, this summarizes the issue of the "Trinity." Clear teachings in the New Covenant prove otherwise:

> *And Yeshua answered him and said, "The first of all the commandments is: Hear O Israel, the Lord our God is one Lord" (Mark 12:29; 1 Corinthians 8:4; James 2:19).*

New Covenant faith is monotheistic; the word "trinity" itself is a contraction of "tri-unity," emphasizing that He is One. But, sadly, confusion prevails because of general ignorance about what is often called "God's mystery nature." This should be clarified where at all possible, not only so that we might better communicate with those who do not yet believe, but that believers themselves might relate to what the Bible says in a Jewish frame of reference. In other words, we need to understand the tri-unity of God is not a Gentile fable or *goyisha bubbemeises*, but revealed truth.

"One" Words

The testimony of the Hebrew Scriptures is the authority for knowing about God, and as we look into *Torah* specifically we see the basis of the Unity of God presented: *"Hear O Israel, the Lord is our God, the Lord is one" (Deuteronomy 6:4).*

Sh'ma Yisrael, Adonai Eloheinu, Adonai echad

One Jewish man commented to me, "God is mentioned three times right there in the verse that speaks of His oneness!" Perhaps, but for now let us notice that the word one (*echad*, in the original Hebrew) can point to a oneness-in-plurality. For example, when God established the marriage relationship, the Scripture states:

For this cause a man shall leave his father and mother and cleave to his wife; and the two shall be <u>one</u> flesh (Genesis 2:24).

Here we see that this word for "one" (*echad*) is not used to indicate something utterly singular, but a oneness-in-plurality. Numbers 13:23 likewise uses the same word to speak of *one* cluster of grapes. And a cluster has a plurality of grapes!

If the Scriptures had wanted to describe God as one in the singular sense with no possibility of a triune nature, there is another word for one in the Hebrew, *yachid*. For instance, *yachid* is used when God was speaking to Abraham about Isaac:

"Take now your son, your <u>only</u> son" (Genesis 22:2).

Although Abraham had another son, Ishmael, God refers to Isaac as a one-of-a-kind son, the son of the covenant (this language prefigures Messiah as shown in Hebrews 11:17; John 3:16).

Yachid is used twelve times in the Hebrew Scriptures, and speaks of a unique or lone oneness (Genesis 22:2, 12, 16; Judges 11:34; Jeremiah 6:26; Amos 8:10; Zechariah 12:10; Psalm 22:20[21]; 25:16; 35:17; 68:6[7]; Proverbs 4:3). However, the word *yachid* is never used regarding God! In light of the rampant polytheism (worship of many gods) in the ancient world, *yachid* would have been useful if the Scriptures were to deny the notion of there being more than one person Who is God. *Yachid* is *never* used in the Bible to describe the Divine nature, and to use it in that way would have been to deny the reality of the triune nature of God.

There is a place where *yachid* is used to describe God - in Maimonides' *Thirteen Principles of Faith.* The third principle, which we looked at in Lesson 8, was written specifically to deny the incarnation of the Messiah, and in historical context, Maimonides' wrote the second principle to deny the triune nature of God. It reads:

I believe with perfect faith that the Creator, blessed be His name, is a Unity, and that there is no unity in any manner like unto His, and that He alone is our God, Who was, is, and will be.

Now, it is certainly true as Maimonides says that the Creator is a Unity; in fact, there is no other unity like His; and indeed, God alone is Eternal. Yet it is interesting that the word used for God's Unity here is *yachid*! Prior to Maimonides, the word *echad* was always used when referring to God's Unity. As the polemical conflict between Rabbinic Judaism and hostile anti-Jewish Christendom worsened, the Rabbinic concept of God strayed from the Bible. Sadly, down to our own day this has led to deep misunderstanding of what the Scriptures teach. Jewish believers in Yeshua are the remnant of the Jewish community that holds to the Biblical view of God.

This nature of God is assumed in the Scripture, rather than explained. That is why a portion like the following one in Genesis can only make sense in light of this assumption:

> *The* LORD *rained upon Sodom brimstone and fire from the* LORD *out of heaven* (Genesis 19:24).

The LORD was on the earth raining down fire and brimstone, also coming from the LORD out of heaven. The Hebrew text presents Him as if there are *two distinct persons,* in *two places at once!*

Even from the first verse of Genesis, it is interesting that the word used for God, *Elohim,* אֱלֹהִים, has a *plural* ending. When God created man, we are brought into the counsels of God's own heart when we read:

> *And God said, "Let Us make man in Our image, according to Our likeness" (Genesis 1:26).*

Notice the plural possessive pronoun "Our." Here God acknowledges *His own plural nature*, as opposed to Him speaking to a group of angels. The Scripture proves this by going on to say:

> *So God created man in His own image, in the image of God He created them; male and female He created them (Genesis 1:27).*

There was no group of "angelic artists" doing the creating: God alone is the Creator, and it is in His image we have been created (body, soul, and spirit, 1 Thessalonians 5:23). So the plural pronoun does not mean there was a group with whom He was speaking or conferring. There were no angels with whom He was consulting, nor does He ever need to (Isaiah 40:13).

Furthermore, the idea that God was declaring the "plurality of majesty" is an idea better suited for Elizabethan England, but you find no king in the Bible using the plurality of majesty. God's nature alone is the reason for the use of the word "Our."

Isaiah the Prophet also assumes this nature of God in several places. In the vision of his own commission as a prophet of Israel, Isaiah writes:

> *Also I heard the voice of the Lord, saying, "Who will go for Us, whom shall We send?" (Isaiah 6:8).*

Once more in God's own counsel, God refers to Himself with a <u>plural</u> pronoun. Isaiah again assumes this unity-in-plurality of God's Nature when he refers to the practical activity of God concerning our redemption:

> *"Come near to Me, hear this: I have not spoken in secret from the beginning; from the time it was, there am I; now the Lord GOD and His Spirit has sent Me" (Isaiah 48:16).*

In Isaiah 48:16, who is the only One who is "from the beginning"?

_____.

Correct - God alone, even as it says in Genesis 1:1, "*in the beginning God created Heaven and earth.*" Also, earlier in the 48th chapter of Isaiah, the Lord says this.

> *"I have declared the former things from the beginning; they went forth from My mouth, and I caused them to hear it. Suddenly I did them, and they came to pass. Even from the beginning I have declared it to you; before it came to pass I proclaimed it to you" (Isaiah 48:3, 5).*

Thus in Isaiah 48:16, it is the Lord Himself ("Me") who is sent by the Lord GOD and His Spirit! Many more portions of the

Hebrew Scriptures address the same truth: There is only One God. Yet this one God is revealed in three Persons: Father (Isaiah 63:16; 64:8), Son (Isaiah 9:5[6]; Proverbs 30:4), and the Holy Spirit (Isaiah 48:16; 63:10; or the Spirit of God, Isaiah 63:14).

In light of the many polytheistic religions surrounding Israel at that time, the Tanakh emphasized the oneness of God, while remaining faithful to the subtle teaching of His plurality. The New Covenant now progressively reveals more of this triune nature (as in Matthew 28:19, *"...immersing them in the name of the Father, the Son and the Holy Spirit..."*), while still being faithful to the truth that there is only one God.

So, the New Covenant reveals the truth of God's triune nature, not to imply that there is more than one God, but to be faithful to the revelation of God's nature as seen in *Tanakh*. The Tri-unity is not a contradiction of the oneness of God, but the best explanation of His oneness.

The Incomparable God

Admittedly, understanding these matters can be difficult, but God's triune nature is better appreciated if we see its application for our lives. To know the Triune God is to know One Who is eternally relational. The Father, the Son, and the Holy Spirit are fully God, and in community with one another. This is how the Eternal God is love - because Father, Son, and Holy Spirit are in eternal fellowship together. This is why Yeshua can say:

> *"By this all men will know that you are My disciples, if you have love for one another" (John 13:35).*

We read from Genesis 1:27 that God made *us* in His image: *"male and female He created them."* Since relationship is intrinsic to the Triune God, it is intrinsic to our lives as well. God created us for relationship with Him and with each other.

We may reflect also on the Son in relationship to the Father. Yeshua the Son always submits to the Father, will never overpower

Him (1 Corinthians 15:28). However, this does not demean the Son, nor does it diminish His nature as God, for He is equal to the Father in nature. So also, within human relationships, there are places for submission, one to another, even in relationships where there are leadership roles (in marriage, families, jobs, and so on). In finding ways to serve one another we thereby imitate the exalted Son (Philippians 2:5-11). This is what we learned in the lesson on Messiah's deity as well: we are to imitate how Messiah humbled Himself.

A famous New Covenant scholar, Augustine of Hippo, was once walking along a beach, trying to understand the Tri-unity of God. As he struggled in thought ("three in one, one in three... *Oy vey!*"), he saw a young boy digging a hole in the seashore and then run back to the ocean over and over taking water from the ocean and pouring it in the hole. Augustine asked him, "Child, what are you doing?"

The boy said, "I'm just trying to put the ocean in this hole!"

Augustine laughed and said to himself, "that's what I was trying to do, too!"

> *"For My thoughts are not your thoughts. For as the heaven is higher than the earth, so My thoughts are higher than your thoughts"* *(Isaiah 55:8-9).*

Mysteries are not like problems to be solved, but rather places where we should fall down to worship. Rather than believe only what we can comprehend, we have faith in God's testimony. We lean not on our own understanding, but rather depend upon the Word (Proverbs 3:5).

Some have used different analogies trying to explain the Triune nature of God. For example, consider a triangle. A triangle is an inseparable unity, yet the triangle is also three angles in relation to each other. Still others have used notions like an egg (which is a yolk, white, and shell), or water (which has three states: gas, liquid, and solid). While analogies can be helpful, we recognize that the reality of God's Being is far beyond any naturally found comparisons. His Unity is truly unique!

In the end, our faith rests on trusting the testimony of Scripture as the true revelation of God; regarding both His nature, and His method of reconciling sinful people to Himself; His free gift of forgiving sins through the atonement in Messiah Yeshua!

Memorize Isaiah 48:16 for your next lesson.

"Come near to Me, hear this: I have not spoken in secret from the beginning; from the time it was, there am I; now the Lord GOD and His Spirit has sent Me."

Give evidence from Old and New Covenant Scripture for the Triune nature of God:

Lesson 11

The Holy Spirit in Salvation

As discussed in the previous chapter, the triune nature of God is revealed in three persons: The Father, the Son, and the Holy Spirit. This is succinctly stated in Matthew 28:19, "...*immersing them in the* <u>*name*</u> *of the Father and of the Son and of the Holy Spirit*" (*Ruach HaKodesh*, רוּחַ הַקֹדֶשׁ, Hebrew for "the Holy Spirit").

In Matthew 28:19 the word name is singular. The New Covenant recognizes the triune nature of God, yet declares that there is only one God. Each of these Persons of the Tri-unity (or Trinity) is instrumental regarding your salvation. The Father planned it before creation (Titus 1:2; Ephesians 1:4; 2 Timothy 1:9), the Son provided it in His sacrificial death (Romans 5:6-8; 1 Corinthians 15:2; Galatians 1:4), and the Holy Spirit applied it when we believed the Good News (Romans 5:5; 8:16; 1 Corinthians 12:13; Ephesians 1:13-14; Titus 3:5).

In the Tanakh, *Ruach HaKodesh* was promised to indwell those who trusted in the Lord:

> *"I will put a new spirit within you; I will take the heart of stone out of your flesh and give you a heart of flesh. I will put <u>My Spirit within you</u> and cause you to walk in My statutes, and you will keep My judgments and do them" (Ezekiel 36:26-27).*

Perhaps the least understood person of the Tri-unity is *Ruach HaKodesh.* There may actually be good reason for this: His work is not to glorify or even bring attention to Himself, but to exalt Yeshua. Yeshua said of the Spirit in John 15:26, *"He will testify of Me."* Yeshua further said:

> *"But when He, the Spirit of truth, comes, He will guide you into all the truth; for He will not speak of Himself, but whatever He hears, He will speak; and He will disclose to you what is to come. He will glorify Me, for He will take of Mine and will disclose it to you." (John 16:13-14).*

The glory of *Ruach HaKodesh* is in bringing glory to Yeshua. So if you're in a fellowship where they are always bringing attention to *HaRuach*, the Spirit, and not Yeshua, such a place is in fact not doing the work of the Spirit, "*...for He shall not speak of Himself, but...He will glorify Me*" *(John 16:13-14)*.

We can also see clearly from these texts that *Ruach HaKodesh* is not merely an impersonal force or influence. One might want to think about the Spirit like "the Force" used in Star Wars, but we should note the pronouns 'He' and 'His'. The Spirit is a Person. Indeed, he has all the qualities of personality:

✡ intelligence (Romans 8:27)

✡ will (1 Corinthians 12:11)

✡ can be grieved (Ephesians 4:30)

✡ resisted (Acts 7:51)

✡ quenched (1 Thessalonians 5:19)

✡ and insulted (Hebrews 10:29).

The Spirit teaches, instructs, leads, and directs (John 16). He can also be:

✡ blasphemed (Luke 12:10)

✡ lied to (Acts 5:3)

✡ and sinned against (Matthew 12:31-32).

The Spirit is God (Romans 8:9; John 14:26; 15:26). As Yeshua is God incarnate (in the flesh), *Ruach HaKodesh* is God indwelling (living in you, John 14:17). The Spirit possesses the qualities of God, for example:

✡ Eternity (Hebrews 9:14)

✡ Omnipotence (Micah 3:8; Romans 15:13)

✡ Omnipresence (Psalm 139:7-10)

✡ Omniscience (1 Corinthians 2:10-11)

✡ Life (Romans 8:2)

✡ Holiness (Matthew 12:31-32)

✡ and Truth (1 John 5:6).

Ruach HaKodesh is timeless, all-powerful, everywhere, all-knowing, living, pure and actually God! Not only does the Spirit have the attributes of God, but He does the works of God as well:

✡ in creation (Genesis 1:2)

✡ regeneration (John 3:8)

✡ resurrection (Romans 8:11)

✡ and receives the honor due God (1 Corinthians 3:16)

✡ because He is equal to God (2 Corinthians 13:14).

Whew! Please take time to think about each of these qualities, reviewing the Holy Spirit's nature and person. It is really worth soaking in!

The Work of the Spirit

You have learned a little about the Holy Spirit's nature. It is now vital that you understand four wonderful works He accomplishes in your life: *regeneration, indwelling, immersion,* and *filling.*

1. The Holy Spirit regenerates you: He makes you alive to God forever! When you trusted in Messiah for your salvation, *Ruach HaKodesh* actually made you spiritually alive to God:

> *But if the Spirit of Him who raised Yeshua from the dead dwells in you, He who raised Messiah from the dead will also give <u>life</u> to your mortal bodies through His Spirit who dwells in you (Romans 8:11).*

Regeneration is receiving the full, free, and forever salvation described in Titus 3:5-6, *"He saved us, through the washing of regeneration and renewing of the Holy Spirit."* This is also called the "new birth" or being "born again" in John 3:6-7, *"That which is born of the Spirit is spirit. Do not marvel that I said to you, 'You must be born again.'"*

In Messiah, all your sins were washed away. You were sanctified, or set apart to God (thus, the Bible says you are a saint!), and made right (justified) with God:

> *But you were <u>washed</u>, but you were <u>sanctified</u>, but you were <u>justified</u> in the name of the Lord Yeshua and by the Spirit of our God (1 Corinthians 6:11).*

What is the tense here of the verbs "washed," "sanctified," and "justified"? Past, Present or Future (circle one).

Yes, they are all in the past tense. That means all of this is already true for you!

2. The Holy Spirit indwells you: You have an Eternal Resource residing within you.

In the Old Covenant, the Spirit came upon believers, and then only temporarily. Hence, King David prayed, *"Do not take Your Holy Spirit from me!"* In the New Covenant, He abides within us permanently (John 14:16; Ephesians 4:30). That is why you are called the Temple of the Holy Spirit (1 Corinthians 6:19-20). By the gracious choice of God, *Ruach HaKodesh* came to indwell you, as opposed to merely be with you.

The resources of the Spirit are illustrated by His titles like Helper and Advocate. Just as Messiah is your Advocate before the Father, pleading His blood for you (1 John 2:1-2), so *Ruach HaKodesh* is the Father's Advocate in you, pleading His love for you. As your indwelling Helper, He is able to intercede as you relate to God in prayer (Romans 8:26-27; Ephesians 6:18; Jude 20).

At salvation, God's love was poured into your heart as *Ruach HaKodesh* came to indwell you forever. *"God's love has been poured into*

our hearts through the Holy Spirit that has been given to us" (Romans 5:5).
At the same time, *Ruach HaKodesh* was given to you and indwelled
you as God's eternal anointing and seal upon you.

> *Now He who establishes us with you in Messiah and has <u>anointed</u>
> <u>us</u> is God, Who also has <u>sealed us</u> and given us the Spirit in our
> hearts as a guarantee (2 Corinthians 1:21-22).*

What is the tense of "anointed" and "sealed"? Past, Present or
Future (circle one).

Yes, they are both in the past tense again. This was true for you
from the moment you trusted in Messiah for your salvation!

"Anointed" (*mashach*, from where we get Mashiach, or Messiah)
is to consecrate for God's purposes, as with the priests in *Tanakh*
(Leviticus 8:12, 30). This anointing in *Ruach HaKodesh* is God's
enablement for you to learn His truths taught in God's word (1 John
2:27). "Sealed" refers to God's eternal guarantee that He will keep
you secure in Messiah's redemption. Paul states:

> *"In Him you also trusted, after you heard the word of truth, the
> Good News of your salvation; in whom also, having believed, you
> were <u>sealed</u> with the Holy Spirit of promise, who is the <u>guarantee</u>
> of our inheritance until the redemption of the purchased possession,
> to the praise of His glory. And do not grieve the Holy Spirit of God,
> by whom you were <u>sealed</u> unto the day of redemption." (Ephesians
> 1:13-14; cf. 4:30; 2 Corinthians 5:5. Notice the past tense)*

This indwelling assures us that neither Satan nor his demons can
possess you. For you are sealed in the all-powerful *Ruach HaKodesh*.
Satan cannot overcome, bind the Spirit of God, or "plunder your
house" (Matthew 12:29; 1 John 4:4). In fact nothing can separate
you from the love of God (Romans 8:37-39).

You are saved with an eternal salvation, based on trusting what
God in Messiah has already done for you, and not on any of your
own works, either to save you or to keep you saved (Galatians 3:2-3).
This doesn't mean you can sin and get away with it, as we shall see in
the next lesson. Nevertheless, it is by the Spirit of God that you are
secure in Him forever.

3. The Holy Spirit immerses you: You are joined with Messiah forever!

When you trusted in Messiah for your salvation, *Ruach HaKodesh* immersed you into the body of Messiah, making you a living member of His spiritual Body. Thus, through the Spirit you are eternally joined to Messiah Yeshua the Lord, which thus joins you to all believers. Consider:

> For <u>by one Spirit we were all immersed into one body</u>—whether Jews or Greeks, whether slaves or free—and have all been made to drink into one Spirit (1 Corinthians 12:13).

According to this verse, into what have all been immersed (or baptized)? "_____ _____".

That's why there is only one body of Messiah, no matter who you are.

According to this verse, how many believers in Yeshua experienced this? "_____".

In fact it must be "all." Otherwise, if you have not been immersed by the Spirit, then you are not a member of His body, and you are not even His! "Now if anyone does not have the Spirit of Messiah, he is not His" (Romans 8:9). But since you have trusted Messiah for your salvation, you are His forever, immersed by the Spirit and joined to the Lord as a living member of His body.

The immersion of Ruac*h HaKodesh* (also called "baptism of the Holy Spirit") makes you a member of the body of Messiah, enabling you to live out Messiah's love and supernaturally empowering you to serve as a member of His body.

According to 1 Corinthians 12:13, what is the tense of "immersed"? Past, Present or Future (circle one).

Yes, it is in the past tense, again (Galatians 3:27; Romans 6:3-4; Colossians 2:11-13; 1 Peter 3:21). This is just what Messiah promised all His followers in Acts 1:5-8: *"you shall be immersed with the*

Holy Spirit... But you shall receive power when the Holy Spirit has come upon you; and you shall be My witnesses in Jerusalem, and in all Judea and Samaria, and to the ends of the earth."

You may have heard of a ceremonial immersion called "baptism." This will be explored in depth in Lesson 14, but for now we should consider that water immersion (or water baptism) is actually meant to picture the Spirit-immersion that took place at salvation. Just as all believers are immersed in the Holy Spirit (the real immersion), so as His disciples, all believers are to be immersed in water (the ritual immersion) in obedience to Messiah (Matthew 28:18-19). Water immersion is a public testimony, a symbol which points to what has been done in saving you. That's why Ephesians 4:5 teaches that there is only "one immersion" for all believers.

Take a short easy test (don't worry - you'll do fine).

Do you believe Messiah Yeshua is your Lord and Savior?

Yes   No   (circle one)

Do you desire to live as His follower?

Yes   No   (circle one)

If your answers are yes, then you may be a candidate for water immersion (see Lesson 14 and speak to your congregational leader).

Even if you have not been water-immersed, the Holy Spirit, upon immersing you into the body of Messiah, "gifted" you, or supernaturally enabled you to serve Him effectively. Thus, the Scriptures teach,

> *There are diversities of gifts, but the same Spirit (1 Corinthians 12:4).*

According to this verse, are all the spiritual gifts alike, or diverse?

_____.

There are many diverse or different gifts. In 1 Peter 4:10-11 it states there are speaking gifts (teaching, exhorting), and serving gifts (helping, mercy, giving). These gifts are often used outside the congregation to reach out, or inwardly so as to edify the body. But in all these gifts, the same Spirit of God manifests the will and work of God in the lives of His people.

To each is given the manifestation of the Spirit for the common good (1 Corinthians 12:7).

According to this verse, why is the gift or the manifestation of the Spirit given?

"...for the _____ good."

Regardless of the particular spiritual gift, the purpose is always the same—for the common good, as opposed to personal, selfish benefit (Acts 8:18-23). As you mature, you will be serving the Lord by His enablement to build up the body and for the common good.

All these (gifts) are activated by one and the same Spirit, who allots to each one individually just as the Spirit chooses (1 Corinthians 12:11).

Who activates, allots and chooses the gifts of the Spirit to each believer? "the same _____, who allots to each one individually just as _____ _____ chooses."

The Spirit of God sovereignly allots and chooses what spiritual gift you receive at the time you were born again and made a member of Messiah's body. As you spiritually mature in Messiah whatever gift you have will perfectly fulfill God's will for you, glorify Him in your life, and bring eternal blessing for you forever.

As you continue to grow, your spiritual gifts will become evident as you yield your life in loving service for the common good and to His Glory. You don't need to seek a spiritual gift. Just seek Him and His glory, and the result will be the *Ruach* living blessedly in and through you!

Remember, you're in a relationship! The Spirit's immersion joins you to Yeshua and is pictured in a variety of ways. Your union to Messiah is like:

✡   A bride to her Husband (see John 3:29; 1 Corinthians 6:17; 2 Corinthians 11:2; Ephesians 5:30-31; Romans 7:4; Revelation 19:7; 21:2). This is a picture of God's love for you.

✡   A body to the head (see Ephesians 1:22-23; 4:15-16; Colossians 1:18; 2:19). This is a picture of God's direction for you.

✡   A branch of a vine (John 15:1-5). This is a picture of God's fruitfulness for you.

✡   Stones of a temple on the strong foundation cornerstone (Ephesians 2:20-22; 1 Peter 2:4-9). This is a picture of God's security for you.

✡   A member of the family (John 1:12; Hebrews 2:10-14). This is a picture of a God's sonship for you.

May these Biblical images minister as you review this lesson, answering the following questions.

1) How do you know that the Holy Spirit is a Person?

2) Describe three works of *Ruach HaKodesh* that took place at your salvation, giving Scriptural support for each.

For your next lesson, please memorize Ephesians 4:30.

Lesson 12

The Holy Spirit in Service

In the last lesson, we considered the nature of *Ruach HaKodesh*, as well as His ministry to you at the moment you trusted in Yeshua for your salvation. Of the four major ministries of *Ruach HaKodesh* impacting all believers' lives, we covered three:

1. Regeneration. You were made spiritually alive to God, born again, a child of God, saved, cleansed of sins, justified, set apart, and so forth.

2. Indwelling. You had God through *Ruach HaKodesh* reside in you, anoint you, seal you, and secure you; so that you could be taught truth, convicted of sin, and know God's love poured out; comforted, helped, and interceded in prayer; and more.

3. Immersing. You were made a member of the body of Messiah, so as to be identified with him and be united with Him.

These three ministries of the Holy Spirit were instantaneous and non-negotiable: your salvation came as the free gift of God by faith in Yeshua. However, the fourth area - the filling of the Spirit - is different. And it is through this function of the Spirit that you live the spiritual life!

Understanding the Filling

The filling of Ruach *HaKodesh* is often misunderstood. Some confuse it with immersion, or even regeneration. The Spirit's indwelling (the Lord in you) and immersion (you in the Lord) is based on your right alignment to Messiah. The Ruach's filling is based on your proper alignment or compliance to the Spirit.

Being saved is you receiving new life from God. Being filled is you living that new life. Salvation is when the Holy Spirit is resident in you; filling is when the Holy Spirit is 'President' of you. When He saved you, you received all of Ruach HaKodesh; when He fills you, He receives all of you, expressing His love through you.

When saved, you are forgiven of all your sins against God. When filled, you are forgiving sins of others against you. Through salvation, God pours out His love into your life. Through filling, God pours out His love through your life to others. Salvation means that God accepted you just as you were. Filling means that you accept others just as they are.

What is the Filling of the Spirit?

In the Scriptures, "to be filled" (Greek: *playro'oh*), is used to mean "to be controlled by" or "under the influence of something or someone else." A few Scriptures will help clarify this:

So all those in the synagogue, when they heard these things, were filled with wrath, and rose up and thrust Him out of the city; and they led Him to the brow of the hill on which their city was built, that they might throw Him down over the cliff (Luke 4:28-29).

Why did they thrust Yeshua out of the city and want to throw Him over a cliff? Because they were filled with wrath, that is, controlled by their wrath.

But they were filled with rage, and discussed with one another what they might do to Yeshua (Luke 6:11).

Similarly, why would religious people want to discuss killing Messiah? They were filled with, that is, controlled by their rage.

But Peter said, "Ananias, why has Satan filled your heart to lie to the Holy Spirit and keep back part of the price of the land for yourself?" (Acts 5:3)

In each case, whatever filled them determined their actions. Whether it was an emotion (like rage) or a person (Satan), to be "filled" then is to be controlled or overpoweringly influenced by whatever or whoever fills the person (Acts 5:17-18; 13:45).

To be filled with the Spirit, therefore, is to be controlled or strongly influenced by the Spirit. This fact is brought out in Ephesians 5:18, *"And do not be drunk with wine, in which is dissipation; but be filled with the Spirit.*" As drunkenness affects behavior for evil, being filled with the Spirit affects a person for good. As a drunken person is under the control of wine, so a filled person is under the control of the Spirit. This does not make you an automaton, without your own will. Rather, you freely comply with the Spirit and His purposes. As you will see, Biblically, this is what it means to be "spiritual."

The Spirit's Directive

The filling of the Spirit is commanded by God. Ephesians was clearly written to believers in Messiah. Yet, in Ephesians 5:18 above, the Greek word translated *"be filled"* is in the imperative, a command for all believers.

Why is there no command for believers to be Spirit-regenerated, indwelled, or immersed? The reason is that spiritual regeneration, indwelling, and immersion is administered to the believer upon faith in Messiah. We were called to trust in Yeshua and be reconciled to God; when this happened, the Lord graciously saved us. However, the same Lord Who saved us commands us now to be filled with the Spirit!

In fact, the command in Ephesians 5:18, *"be filled,"* is a present imperative, meaning "stay filled." Why would the Scripture need to tell believers to stay filled? Because, the filling of *Ruach HaKodesh* is different than His other works in your life. Yes, like His other works, they are about depending on His perfect faithfulness toward you. However, the first three are permanent and once-for-all (Hebrews 7:24-28). Yet, in the Scriptures, the filling of the Holy Spirit is evidently a repeated activity. This is true even for the Apostles!

> *All of them were filled with the Holy Spirit and began to speak ... (Acts 2:4).*

> *Then Peter, filled with the Holy Spirit, said to them... (Acts 4:8).*

> *And when they had prayed, the place where they were assembled together was shaken; and they were all filled with the Holy Spirit, and they spoke the word of God with boldness (Acts 4:31).*

Paul, too, was repeatedly filled with the Spirit (Acts 9:17; 13:9). But why would there be repeated fillings of the Spirit? Because, first, it depended on *the Spirit's purpose*, and, second, it depended on *the believer's compliance*. Sometimes the Spirit wanted Paul to be quite passionate, and other times He wanted Paul to be rather analytical. This is seen even in his writing style, for example, his passion in 2 Corinthians, or his extended argumentation in Romans. God's purposes can vary as He expresses Himself through you as well. You only need to comply with His purposes for your life.

To be Spiritual, Not Just a "Believer"

You may wonder, "Can a believer be non-compliant with the Ruach and still be a real believer?" Yes, in fact, people can be regenerate yet not be filled with the Spirit. The Scripture deals extensively with this subject. To better understand an aspect of our compliance and being filled with Ruach HaKodesh, please read through the following portion:

> *But a <u>natural person</u> does not accept the things of the Spirit of God, for they are foolishness to him; and he cannot understand them, because they are spiritually appraised. But <u>the spiritual person</u> appraises all things, yet he himself is appraised by no one. For "Who has known the mind of the Lord, that he will instruct Him"? But we have the mind of Messiah. And I, brethren, could not speak to you as to spiritual people but as to <u>men of flesh</u>, as to infants in Messiah. I gave you milk to drink, not solid food; for you were not yet able to receive it. Indeed, even now you are not yet able, for you are still fleshly. For since there is jealousy and strife among you, are you not fleshly, and are you not walking like mere men? (1 Corinthians 2:14-3:3)*

In this section of Scripture, we see three states in which people may find themselves:

a) Natural - non-believers (2:14)

b) Spiritual - compliant believers (2:15-16)

c) Fleshly - non-compliant believers (3:1-3)

Natural people are those whose hearts and minds have not yet been indwelled by the Holy Spirit. In the natural, we understand and live life from a merely human frame of reference. Things of God - the "supernatural" - are meaningless to a natural perspective.

Spiritual people are believers in Yeshua who understand and live life from a Biblical frame of reference in compliance with the Spirit. Though this is not "unnatural" - living how one was created to live is never unnatural - it may seem that way to those outside the faith. Because they comply with the Spirit, these believers are described as spiritual. They are victorious and have God's joy (Galatians 5:22).

What about fleshly people, then? These are believers in Yeshua, who understand and live life from a frame of reference in non-compliance with the Spirit, which is why they are described as fleshly. These are believers, but without God's joy.

Believers are spiritual, not simply by being believers, but by complying with the Spirit. Otherwise, we are complying with our "flesh," which does not refer to merely your physical body, but your own self-serving attitudes. So for true "spirituality," you must yield to God's direction in your life that His will might be revealed in you daily (Romans 12:2; 2 Corinthians 4:11).

According to 1 Corinthians 2:14, what are natural people unable to accept? They cannot accept the _____ ____ _____ _____ of God.

"The things of the Spirit of God" refers to all the spiritual truths regarding the nature of man, the evil of sin, the grace of God, the life and sacrifice of Yeshua, and so forth. According to 1 Corinthians 2:14, why can't natural people accept the things of the Spirit of God? Because they are _____ _____.

The filling of the Spirit gives you the perspective of the Lord, for you are actually *yielding* your life *to* His perspective on matters that impact your life. This is why according to 1 Corinthians 2:15, a *"spiritual person appraises all things, yet he himself is appraised by no one."*

According to 1 Corinthians 3:2, as "infants" what was the only thing, that they could receive?

_____ to drink, not _____ _____.

When we are fleshly we are yielding to our own wills, like babies, unable to appreciate anything but milk - the simplest truths of what God has done for us. So also we are unable to stomach or receive meat, that is, to apply and live out the truth by caring for those around us instead of ourselves (Hebrews 5:11-14).

According to 1 Corinthians 3:3, what results from a fleshly believer's interaction with others? There is _____ _____ _____ among you.

Like babies unwilling to share their toys, those who are fleshly exhibit jealousy and strife. They are filled with their flesh, and out of the will of God.

What the Spiritual Life Looks Like

When we are filled with the Spirit we:

- walk by the Spirit—live your daily life in His will and by His power (Galatians 5:25).

- pray in the Spirit—pray for God's will to be done (Ephesians 6:18; Philippians 3:3; Jude 20), even when you do not know the details of His will (Romans 8:26-27).

- are taught by the Spirit (1 Corinthians 2:14; 1 John 2:27).

- are led by the Spirit—to do those things which please God, like repenting for fleshly attitudes and activities (Romans 8:13-14).

In short, the life you are living is God's life (Galatians 2:20).

The evidence of the Spirit-filled life is called the fruit of the Spirit - it is the result of His working in and through you. The fruit of the Spirit reflects the characteristics of God, seen in those who live in compliance with His Spirit - that's called godliness. As it states in Galatians 5:22-23, *"the fruit of the Spirit is love, joy, peace, patience, kindness, goodness, faithfulness, gentleness, self-control."* Living out these qualities of God has nothing to do with particular spiritual gifts, denominations or congregations. It has to do with compliance to the Spirit.

Scriptural commands express how to be filled with the Spirit:

a) Grieve not the Spirit (Ephesians 4:30)

b) Quench not the Spirit (1 Thessalonians 5:19)

c) Walk in the Spirit (Galatians 5:16).

Do not grieve the Spirit. The Spirit grieves when a believer sins, because He knows the reality of what sin does both in the believer and in the believer's relationship to Him (Psalm 32:1-8). In short, He knows the grief of sin before we do. He grieves until we confess and repent from our rebellion toward Him. The first step to being filled with the *Ruach* is to repent of all sin and to accept cleansing in the blood of Yeshua (1 John 1:7, 9).

Do not quench the Spirit. The Spirit is 'quenched' (or stifled) when His prompting to yield and respond to God's word is not heeded. Those who confessed their sins are cleansed but now need to yield to the Spirit and to stop suppressing or resisting Him. For instance, when you know He wants you to apologize to another person, do not resist His godly urging with fleshly excuses. Instead you are to yield to the *Ruach* and subordinate your will to His will, even as Yeshua did (Luke 22:42).

Walk in the Spirit. To "walk in the Spirit" is not merely obedience, but full dependence on the Spirit of God. Consciously depend on His power, *"for it is God who is at work in you, both to will and to work for His good pleasure" (Philippians 2:13).* God provides all the power you need to do His will for His glory (Romans 8:37; Philippians 4:13). As we walk in the Spirit we are enabled to love, forgive, and be humble, or even bold, in ways that go beyond our personalities.

Being filled with the Spirit is living the spiritual life as a spiritually compliant person. This manifests God's fellowship with you as you walk humbly with your God.

> *He has shown thee, O man, what is good; and what does the LORD require of thee, but to do justly, and to love mercy, and to walk humbly with thy God? (Micah 6:8)*

In doing these things you are filled with *Ruach HaKodesh*! This is the spiritual life: now go live it!

Please answer the following questions:

1) How is the filling of the Spirit different from immersion by the Spirit?

2) How are you filled by Ruach HaKodesh ?

Memorize 1 Thessalonians 5:19, and Galatians 5:16.

PART 4

Basic Symbols

Lesson 13

The Lord's Supper (*Zikkaron*)

There are many symbols in the Scripture which point us to Messiah. However, as far as those commanded for New Covenant believers, Messiah gave us two which ceremonially testify of Him: *Zikkaron* (Remembrance) and *tevilah* (Immersion).

Tevilah and *Zikkaron* both represent aspects of our salvation. *Tevilah* is done only once for it represents the once-for-all salvation a believer has in Yeshua (Ephesians 4:5). *Zikkaron* is regularly celebrated, since it represents the continuing testimony of Messiah's saving atonement for our sins. Both were instituted by the commands of the Lord (Matthew 28:19; 1 Corinthians 11:23-26). This chapter will consider the Biblical issues regarding *Zikkaron*.

The Origins of *Zikkaron*

Zikkaron is the Hebrew word for "remembrance" or memorial (Numbers 10:10). Today in Israel, *Yom HaZikkaron* ("Memorial Day") is a day in which those are remembered who have fallen in battle. Since Messiah commanded believers to partake of the bread and cup *"in remembrance of Me,"* we use the term *Zikkaron* for this on-going ceremony (Luke 22:19).

Also called the Lord's Supper or communion, *Zikkaron* was instituted by Yeshua while celebrating Passover with His disciples (Matthew 26:26-28, Mark 14:22-24). The feast of Passover is a yearly reminder of God's redemption of His people from Egyptian bondage (Exodus 12).

Yeshua used the third cup, traditionally called the Cup of Redemption, to represent Himself in the *seder* meal. At Passover, the blood of the lamb kept judgment from our people, as God said, *"when I see the blood I will pass over you" (Exodus 12:13).* Yeshua initiated the New Covenant in His blood as a picture of the fullness of this redemption (Jeremiah 31:31-34; Luke 22:20).

Messiah also used a special piece of unleavened bread, or *matzah*. The *Afikomen* is the piece of unleavened bread traditionally hidden before and then found after the meal, even as the lamb was sacrificed before the meal and deliverance from Egypt followed after that first Passover meal. Messiah utilized this unleavened *Afikomen* to represent His sinless sacrifice for our deliverance (Luke 22:19). The partakers in this bread identify with the true freedom from sin that God has provided for all who will believe in Yeshua.

Therefore, rooted in the Passover remembrance of redemption, the bread and cup are ongoing symbols of the final atoning sacrifice for sin in Messiah's death and resurrection.

Approaching *Zikkaron*

Paul gives more detail about *Zikkaron* in his first letter to the Corinthians (1 Corinthians 11:17-34). *"For as often as you eat this bread and drink this cup, you proclaim the Lord's death till He comes" (11:26).* What is the significance of the phrase *"till He comes"*? When Yeshua returns, we will no longer need the symbols, for the Reality will be with us! That is why it is for believers only—a testimony of faith in Yeshua's death, resurrection, and return.

Paul rebuked the Corinthians' abuse of *Zikkaron*, for not sharing fellowship in the Lord and even hoarding the wine to get drunk (11:21). By contrast, *Zikkaron* should be partaken after we examine ourselves individually.

The Bible generally encourages a 'forward focused' attitude, and not a kind of a morbid introspection. Thus, times when the Scriptures do direct self-examination are noteworthy (Philippians 3:8-14; 1 Corinthians 4:3-5). *Zikkaron* is such a place. To partake of the Lord's Supper in an unworthy manner—with unconfessed sin in our lives, an irreverent attitude, or as mere ritual—is to go against the very One whom *Zikkaron* proclaims. If there is anything defiling in our souls, we are to confess it to God, and be cleansed through Messiah's finished work. Then we may partake of *Zikkaron*.

Zikkaron and Messiah

Various threads of *Tanakh* come together to give a picture of what the Lord instituted at *Zikkaron*. As already mentioned, it is a picture of the Passover hope—the redemption and new life provided through Messiah, our Passover lamb (John 1:29; 1 Corinthians 5:7, 1 Peter 1:18-19).

In Isaiah 53, prophesying a future confession by national Israel, Messiah's death is recognized as an offering for our sins:

> But the LORD was pleased to crush Him, putting Him to grief; if He would render Himself as <u>a guilt offering</u>, He will see His off-spring, He will prolong His days, and the good pleasure of the LORD will prosper in His hand. As a result of the anguish of His soul, He will see it and be satisfied; by His knowledge the Righteous One, My Servant, will justify the many, as He will bear their iniquities. Therefore, I will allot Him a portion with the great, and He will divide the spoil with the strong; because <u>He poured out Himself to death</u>, and was numbered with the transgressors; yet He Himself bore the sin of many, and interceded for the transgressors (Isaiah 53:10-12).

Isaiah presents Messiah's sacrifice in two ways: as a guilt offering (Leviticus 4-5), and as one who has poured out Himself to death—that is, as the drink offering which accompanied most sacrifices (Genesis 35:14; Exodus 37:16).

There are different Hebrew words for "pour out," their meanings are illuminating. The most common word is *nasach*, from which we get the noun "a drink offering" (Numbers 28:7). But in Isaiah 53:12 the word is *'arah* which means to pour so as to empty out completely. Messiah would pour out Himself as a drink offering till there was nothing left, even unto death. In light of this verse, the New Covenant proclaims the fulfillment of this promise as Messiah speaks of His own sacrificial death:

> And He said to them, "This is My blood of the covenant, which is <u>poured out</u> for many" (Mark 14:24).

And in the same way He took the cup after they had eaten, saying, "This cup which is <u>poured out</u> for you is the new covenant in My blood" (Luke 22:20).

The *asham* or trespass/guilt offering was always to be a blood sacrifice for the atonement of sins. So one might expect *Zikkaron* to be meat and cup, rather than bread and cup. But the Scriptures teach if a person was too poor to provide a lamb or even two birds, then they were to take flour and use it on the altar for their sacrifice.

But if his means are insufficient for two turtledoves or two young pigeons, then for his offering for that which he has sinned, he shall bring the tenth of an ephah of fine flour for a sin offering. He shall bring it to the priest, and the priest shall take his handful of it as its memorial portion and offer it up in smoke <u>on the altar, with the offerings</u> of the LORD by fire: it is a sin offering (Leviticus 5:11-12).

Please notice the "fine flour" (meal offering) was placed on the altar, with the offerings (*'al ishei*, "upon the burnt offering"). The meal offering was always identified with the bloody and effective sacrifice for sin. *Zikkaron* reminds us that even the poorest can come to God by identifying with the blood atonement of Messiah. Isaiah 53 wonderfully pictures the Lord's Supper for all who believe in Yeshua and "proclaim His death until He comes."

The Nature of the Elements

Both elements, the bread and the cup, are vitally important. The bread reminds us that He gave His body as payment for the sin debt we owed God (2 Corinthians 5:21; Hebrews 10:5-10) Through His sacrifice we have forgiveness from God. The cup reminds us of His blood which cleanses the stain of sin (1 John 1:7). Through the shedding of his blood, we have fellowship with God.

There has been some confusion among the body of Messiah regarding the nature of the elements. Some traditions teach that the symbols are a real sacrifice: that is, the bread and cup actually become Messiah's literal body and blood, and contain efficacy for forgiveness (sacrament). The Bible does not teach this.

Rather, the Scriptures teach that *Zikkaron* is a symbolic reminder of His once and for all sacrifice for sins (Hebrews 10:11-18). All spiritual efficacy is received when faith is placed in Yeshua and His final atonement for sins. *Zikkaron* reminds us of what He has done for us in the past, which will be spiritually effective for us forever (Revelation 5:9)!

The Contents of *Zikkaron*

Since different believers celebrate it at different times, some wonder, "How frequently is *Zikkaron* to be celebrated?" Yeshua said, *"as often as you eat this bread."* So, while we know it is to be repeated, there is no prescribed frequency in the Scripture. Because it was established at Passover (and the words "this bread" refer originally to Passover *matzah*), some choose to observe it only on Passover. Others do it daily, weekly, or monthly.

Questions also are raised regarding the contents of the bread and cup. The bread is best represented by *matzah*, or unleavened bread, even as Messiah was without sin (leaven is a Biblical picture of sin, 1 Corinthians 5:6-8). Red wine (or grape juice for some fellowships) is used to represent the blood of the Lamb. What is most important are not the elements themselves, but the reality of Messiah's love and sacrifice to which the symbols point.

Lesson 14

Immersion

(*Tevilah* or *Mikveh*)

Submitted disciples follow Messiah's commandments, which include the act of immersion:

> *And Yeshua came up and spoke to them, saying, "All authority has been given to Me in heaven and on earth. Go therefore and make disciples of all the nations, immersing them in the name of the Father, and of the Son, and of the Holy Spirit" (Matthew 28:18-19).*

This teaching on immersion, rounding out this study, is written for your edification, *"for the goal of our instruction is love" (1 Timothy 1:5).* By seeing the meaning and purpose of this symbol, our hope is that you will make it part of your discipleship as well.

Terminology

"Immerse" is a translation of the Greek word, *baptizo*, which is sometimes transliterated as "baptize," but the concept has always been a part of Judaic tradition. When the Rabbis translated the Hebrew Scriptures into the Greek Septuagint, *bapto*, the root of "baptize," was the word used for *taval*, meaning "to dip" or "to plunge" (Exodus 12:22; 2 Kings 5:14; Job 9:31). Both Hebrew translations of the New Covenant and Rabbinic traditional customs use this word *taval* for "baptize." We will use *tevilah* (from *taval*) as this is commonly used among Israeli believers to refer to immersion.

Another Hebrew word used for immersion is *mikveh*, meaning "reservoir" or "collected water," as in a cistern (Exodus 7:19; Leviticus 11:36). The word *mikveh* was utilized in Judaism from the Second Temple period, or the time of Yeshua, to refer to ceremonial cleansing (Leviticus 14-15). So also in Judaism today, many complex laws have been built up around the practice. Many Messianic Jews use the term *mikveh* for immersion.

The original intent of *tevilah* as a concept implied being submerged into the water. As noted, the word baptism is the transliteration of the Greek word *baptizo*, meaning "to dip, immerse, plunge, or wash" (Mark 7:4; Luke 11:38). This term was used in the textile trade for dyeing clothes (one would "baptize" them in dye), and would also describe a sunken ship. Thus when *tevilah* was Biblically practiced it was, for this reason, always near "much water" (John 3:23).

Significance of *Tevilah*

The symbolism of the immersion service is a picture of what was spiritually accomplished when you came to faith in Yeshua. As we recall from earlier lessons, at that instant you were immersed by the Spirit of God into the Body of Yeshua and His death. This is when your sins were truly removed. When you came to faith in Yeshua you died to sin as a way of life.

Notice how Paul pictures the salvation experience through the imagery of immersion:

> *What shall we say then? Are we to continue in sin so that grace may abound? May it never be! How shall we who died to sin still live in it? Or do you not know that all of us who have been immersed into Messiah Yeshua have been immersed into His death?*
> *(Romans 6:3)*

Tevilah pictures us identifying publicly with Messiah's death, even as the spirit-immersion identified us internally with Messiah's death. When you trusted in Yeshua you were spiritually immersed into the body of Yeshua, as well as cleansed of your sins by His atonement. Since immersion is a picture of burial, consider this principle: the ritual of burial (immersion) follows death (to sin); it never precedes death.

> *Therefore we have been buried with Him through immersion into death, so that as Messiah was raised from the dead through the glory of the Father, so we too might walk in newness of life (Romans 6:4).*

Coming up out of the water is like your being raised up with Messiah. Walking out of the water illustrates your walking with Him in the newness of life, even His resurrection life!

The immersion service pictures our identifying unity with Messiah in death and resurrection:

> *For if we have become united with Him in the likeness of His death, certainly we shall also be in the likeness of His resurrection. Knowing this, that our old self was crucified with Him, in order that our body of sin might be done away with, so that we would no longer be slaves to sin (Romans 6:5-6).*

By the spiritually effective immersion in the Holy Spirit (*Tevilah b'Ruach HaKodesh*), you were spiritually crucified with Yeshua. You acknowledge by faith in Messiah that He took your place in judgment for sins. By that same faith in Yeshua, you therefore no longer live as a slave to sin: you have new life in Messiah!

Tevilah and *Mikveh* in Jewish Tradition

Tevilah originated out of the Scriptural customs regarding ceremonial cleansing from impurity (leprosy, Leviticus 14; emissions and menstruation, Leviticus 15). The water that Messiah turned into wine was set apart for this purpose, "*for the Jewish custom of purification*" *(John 2:6).*

Ceremonial cleansing was also required of *cohenim* (priests) upon entering the priesthood (Leviticus 8:6). Proselytes to Judaism still go through *mikveh* and circumcision. Immersion is considered an outward sign of an inward reality of true spiritual cleansing and commitment.

We see from the Talmud,

> *Rabbi Akiva said: "Happy are you, Israel! Before whom do you make yourselves tahor (clean), and who makes you tahor? Your Father in Heaven. As it is written, 'The Mikveh of Israel is the LORD' (Jeremiah 17:13). Just as the mikveh makes tahor those who are tameh (unclean), so the Holy One makes Israel tahor" (Mishnah Yoma 8:9).*

Who is to be Immersed?

The only people who are to be immersed (or baptized) are believers in Yeshua, making *tevilah* one of the first steps of being His disciple. There is no Biblical teaching to immerse infants or anyone else who has not yet professed personal faith in Yeshua.

One Scripture occasionally brought forward in favor of infant immersion (or baptism) is Acts 16:31-33:

> *They said, "Believe in the Lord Jesus, and you will be saved, you and your household." And they spoke the word of the Lord to him together with all who were in his house. And he took them that very hour of the night and washed their wounds, and immediately he was immersed, he and all his household.*

The wrong interpretation of this verse comes from the assumption that because it mentions "household," there must be an infant involved. Yet no infant is mentioned in the text.

Also, we must not assume that "you and your household" means that if one believes, the whole family is saved. This is unfortunately not true, even as Messiah prophesies of a time in which *"brother will betray brother to death, and a father his child; and children will rise up against parents and cause them to be put to death" (Matthew 10:21).*

Yes, an entire family can be saved, but each one must believe the Good News for himself. In the Acts 16 passage above, we see that the entire family had the Good News presented to them. Evidently they all believed, for then they all were immersed, with no mention of infants.

Immersion, therefore, is a testimony for professing believers only.

When to get Immersed

Though there is no waiting period required for *tevilah*, there is the implied Biblical expectation that the believer will know in Whom they have believed.

A candidate is not only one who believes and confesses that Yeshua is Messiah, Lord and Savior, but also understands the meaning and commitment of *tevilah*. Even as the Scripture states, *"immersing them in the Name of the Father and the Son and the Holy Spirit,"* so also they are to know there is only one God ("in the Name" --singular), and that He is Triune in Nature ("the Father, and the Son, and the Holy Spirit").

One should understand the Bible's teaching of personal sin and judgment, Messiah's atoning death, resurrection and forgiveness by faith, Messiah's deity, and the triune nature of God. This is quite a full plate, but we are not talking about mature understanding, which will come in time, but an introductory understanding and trust in Messiah about these vital matters.

Tevilah follows salvation and does not play a part in making someone saved, or more fully saved. Salvation comes only by grace through faith in Yeshua's finished work of salvation (Ephesians 2:8-9; Romans 4:9-13). We are saved by faith in Messiah's work, not by our own works.

To illustrate this, there is one person in Scripture who was personally promised salvation by Yeshua and yet was never, and could never be, immersed: the thief on the cross next to Yeshua.

> ...[the thief] was saying, "Yeshua, remember me when You come in Your kingdom!"

> And He said to him, "Truly I say to you, today you shall be with Me in Paradise" (Luke 23:42-43).

The thief died before leaving the cross, yet Yeshua guaranteed him salvation based on his simple trust in Him as the King who could bring him into His heavenly kingdom. Ritual immersion, therefore, has nothing to do with saving someone.

The fact that water baptism does not save is the reason why Paul paid it less attention compared to the Good News. Paul writes,

> I thank God that I immersed none of you except Crispus and Gaius,

so that no one would say you were immersed in my name. Now I did immerse also the household of Stephanas; beyond that, I do not know whether I immersed any other. For Messiah did not send me to immerse, but to preach the Good News (1 Corinthians 1:14–17).

Since Paul would not have neglected to do anything that would leave people unsaved, why would he leave them unimmersed? It is because immersion is not part of the saving gospel that he was called to preach. *Tevilah* followed salvation, and Paul left that to the other leaders. We are saved by faith in Yeshua.

There are some groups that claim Acts 2:38 teaches salvation comes through immersion: *"Peter said to them, 'Repent, and each of you be immersed in the name of Messiah Yeshua for the forgiveness of your sins.'"*

The word "repent" in the Greek is an imperative; which means that it is a command to respond to immediately. These words "for the forgiveness of your sins" deserve very careful consideration. The question revolves around whether "for" means "in order to gain forgiveness," or, whether it means "because you are already forgiven." The word "for" can be used either way in English as in the original language. If a reward poster read, *"Billy the Kid: Wanted for Murder,"* no one would think it is a job opportunity for Billy! The reward is offered because he already murdered.

In the Scripture, Peter is urging immersion upon each of them who had already turned (repented) and thus received the forgiveness of sins by faith in Yeshua. Therefore, the verse can read: *"Repent, and each of you be baptized in the name of Messiah Yeshua because of the forgiveness of your sins."*

Immersion is a public testimony, like a witness' testimony in court for an incident that has already occurred. We testify of Messiah, taking our stand with Him. Thus, *tevilah* is a vital act of obedience to Messiah. It testifies of one's faith and salvation in Yeshua, and is in fact the normal testimony of all believers, and the natural expectation for those who are growing in Him.

How to Immerse

The immersed believer is publicly confessing to being Yeshua's disciple and committing to follow Him daily. The candidate must understand that *tevilah* does not save nor perfect the believer, but is an act of obedience and confession of faith in Yeshua.

Attire may vary from robes to bathing suits, but modesty is always required. Usually men and women will wear at least a tee shirt over their bathing suits.

At the side of the tank or pool, the believer usually will share a short testimony of faith before entering the water.

Once in the water, the believer walks to the leader, and stands at a right angle to him. The leader may ask questions of the candidate so that their testimony of faith is clearly expressed:

"When Yeshua died for sins, did He die for *your* sins?"

"Do you believe He was raised bodily from the dead?"

"Will you willingly follow Him as your Lord and Messiah?"

The leader will place his right hand on the believer's upper back, and the believer will pinch his nose with his right hand and hold his right wrist with his left hand.

The leader will then place his left hand over the believer's hands. The leader then prays:

> *Baruch Atah Adonai Eloheinu Melech ha'olam, asher vitsivanu al hatevilah. Blessed are You, Lord our God, King of the universe, who has commanded us concerning immersion.*

He then declares,

> *According to your confession of faith in Messiah Yeshua and by the authority of the word of God, I immerse you my sister/brother in the Name of the Father, the Son and the Holy Spirit (b'Shem ha'Av, ha'Ben, v'Ruach haKodesh).*

The leader will gently lower the believer backward into the water until his head is just submerged and then will raise her/him upright (note: other provisions are made for those with disabilities). The believer may be prayed for at that time or following the immersion of any others. The believer then walks out of the water, dries off, and receives lots of hugs and *Mazel Tov*'s!

Both *Zikkaron* and *tevilah* are beautiful opportunities for Messianic believers to identify with, testify to, and faithfully honor Messiah as they fellowship together in Him. Please answer the following questions regarding *Zikkaron* and *tevilah*.

1. How did *Zikkaron* and *tevilah* originate and how do they represent our salvation?

2. Will either of them save you? Please explain why or why not.

3. Who may participate in *Zikkaron* and *tevilah*, and why?

4. Do you have any (further) questions about *Zikkaron* and *tevilah*?

Yeshua said, *"If you know these things blessed are you that do them"* *(John 13:17)*. Always remember: the blessing is in the doing! While the information provided in this book can be helpful for you insofar as it reflects the Scriptures, discipleship takes place when we implement it, share it, and live it out. May the Lord bless you and keep you in your journey. (You can find further resources on page 118.)

"The LORD bless you and keep you

The LORD make His face shine on you,

and be gracious to you;

The LORD lift up His countenance on you,

and give you peace"

(Numbers 6:24-26)

✡✡✡✡✡✡✡✡✡✡

Appendix A - The Books of the Bible

The *Tanakh* and (Protestant) "Old Testament" have the same books, but they are arranged in different orders. We recommend you memorize in the order that corresponds to your Bible.

Tanakh (Hebrew order)

Torah	Genesis *(Bereishit)* Exodus *(Shemot)* Leviticus *(Vayikra)* Numbers *(Bamidbar)* Deuteronomy *(Devarim)*
Nevi'im "Former Prophets" "The Book of the Twelve"	Joshua, Judges, 1 Samuel, 2 Samuel, 1 Kings, 2 Kings, Isaiah, Jeremiah, Ezekiel, Hosea, Joel, Amos, Obadiah, Jonah, Micah, Nahum, Habakkuk, Zephaniah, Haggai, Zechariah, Malachi.
Ketuvim "The Megillot"	Psalms *(Tehillim)*, Proverbs *(Mishlei)*, Job, Song of Songs, Ruth, Lamentations, Ecclesiastes, Esther, Daniel, Ezra, Nehemiah, 1 Chronicles, 2 Chronicles.

Old Covenant Scriptures (Greek order)

Torah (Pentateuch)	Genesis Exodus Leviticus Numbers Deuteronomy
History	Joshua, Judges, Ruth, 1 Samuel, 2 Samuel, 1 Kings, 2 Kings, 1 Chronicles, 2 Chronicles, Ezra, Nehemiah, Esther, Job,
Wisdom Literature	Psalms, Proverbs, Ecclesiastes, Song of Songs
Prophets	Isaiah, Jeremiah, Lamentations, Ezekiel, Daniel, Hosea, Joel, Amos, Obadiah, Jonah, Micah, Nahum, Habakkuk, Zephaniah, Haggai, Zechariah, Malachi.

New Covenant Scriptures (*Brit Chadashah*)

Good News Accounts or "Gospels"	Matthew 　　Mark 　　　　Luke 　　　　　John
History Letters	Acts of the Apostles Romans, 1 and 2 Corinthians Galatians, Ephesians, Philippians, Colossians, 1 and 2 Thessalonians, 1 and 2 Timothy, Titus, Philemon, Hebrews, James, 1 and 2 Peter, 1, 2, and 3 John, Jude Revelation

- There are 39 books in the *Tanakh* and 27 books in the New Covenant Scriptures.

- *Tanakh* is an acrostic of *Torah*, *Nevi'im* (Prophets), and *Ketuvim* (Writings).

- The "Greek" order refers to the order derived from the Septuagint, an ancient Greek translation of the *Tanakh*.

- Torah means "(divine) instruction," so all Scripture can be considered Torah. However, it refers here to the first five books, also called the Pentateuch (*penta*=five; *teuch*=book).

- Books which are found in two or three parts (1 Samuel, 2 Kings, 3 John) are said as "first" "second" and "third."

Appendix B - Prophecies of the Messiah

"We have found Him of whom Moses in the Law and also the Prophets spoke – Yeshua of Nazareth" (John 1:45)

Subject	Old Covenant	New Covenant
A descendent of Abraham	*Genesis 12:3*	*Matthew 1:1* *Galatians 3:8*
Of the Tribe of Judah	*Genesis 49:10*	*Luke 3:33*
Heir of King David	*Isaiah 9:7*	*Luke 1:32*
He was to come before the destruction of the Temple	*Malachi 3:1* *Daniel 9:26*	*Matthew 24:1*
He was to be born in Bethlehem	*Micah 5:2(1)*	*Luke 2:4-7*
Born of a virgin	*Isaiah 7:14*	*Matthew 1:23*
A ministry in Galilee	*Isaiah 9:1(8:23)*	*Matthew 4:13-16*
Son of God	*Psalm 2:7,12*	*Matthew 3:17*
He is God in the flesh	*Isaiah 9:6(5); 10:21*	*Hebrews 1:8-12*
Preceded by a fore-runner	*Isaiah 40:3* *Malachi 3:1*	*Mark 1:2-4*
Initially rejected by His people	*Isaiah 53:3*	*John 1:11*
He was to be an atonement for sins	*Isaiah 53:6* *Daniel 9:24-26*	*Matthew 20:28*
He was resurrected	*Psalm 16:10*	*Luke 24:6-7*
He will be accepted	*Zechariah 12:10*	*Revelation 1:7*

‏52:13 הִנֵּה יַשְׂכִּיל עַבְדִּי יָרוּם וְנִשָּׂא וְגָבַהּ מְאֹד׃

‏52:14 כַּאֲשֶׁר שָׁמְמוּ עָלֶיךָ רַבִּים כֵּן־מִשְׁחַת מֵאִישׁ מַרְאֵהוּ
וְתֹאֲרוֹ מִבְּנֵי אָדָם׃

‏52:15 כֵּן יַזֶּה גּוֹיִם רַבִּים עָלָיו יִקְפְּצוּ מְלָכִים פִּיהֶם
כִּי אֲשֶׁר לֹא־סֻפַּר לָהֶם רָאוּ וַאֲשֶׁר לֹא־שָׁמְעוּ הִתְבּוֹנָנוּ׃

‏53:1 מִי הֶאֱמִין לִשְׁמֻעָתֵנוּ וּזְרוֹעַ יְהוָה עַל־מִי נִגְלָתָה׃

‏53:2 וַיַּעַל כַּיּוֹנֵק לְפָנָיו וְכַשֹּׁרֶשׁ מֵאֶרֶץ צִיָּה
לֹא־תֹאַר לוֹ וְלֹא הָדָר
וְנִרְאֵהוּ וְלֹא־מַרְאֶה וְנֶחְמְדֵהוּ׃

‏53:3 נִבְזֶה וַחֲדַל אִישִׁים אִישׁ מַכְאֹבוֹת וִידוּעַ חֹלִי
וּכְמַסְתֵּר פָּנִים מִמֶּנּוּ נִבְזֶה וְלֹא חֲשַׁבְנֻהוּ׃

‏53:4 אָכֵן חֳלָיֵנוּ הוּא נָשָׂא וּמַכְאֹבֵינוּ סְבָלָם
וַאֲנַחְנוּ חֲשַׁבְנֻהוּ נָגוּעַ מֻכֵּה אֱלֹהִים וּמְעֻנֶּה׃

‏53:5 וְהוּא מְחֹלָל מִפְּשָׁעֵנוּ מְדֻכָּא מֵעֲוֺנֹתֵינוּ
מוּסַר שְׁלוֹמֵנוּ עָלָיו וּבַחֲבֻרָתוֹ נִרְפָּא־לָנוּ׃

‏53:6 כֻּלָּנוּ כַּצֹּאן תָּעִינוּ אִישׁ לְדַרְכּוֹ פָּנִינוּ
וַיהוָה הִפְגִּיעַ בּוֹ אֵת עֲוֺן כֻּלָּנוּ׃

נִגַּשׂ וְהוּא נַעֲנֶה וְלֹא יִפְתַּח־פִּיו כַּשֶּׂה לַטֶּבַח יוּבָל 53:7
וּכְרָחֵל לִפְנֵי גֹזְזֶיהָ נֶאֱלָמָה וְלֹא יִפְתַּח פִּיו:

מֵעֹצֶר וּמִמִּשְׁפָּט לֻקָּח וְאֶת־דּוֹרוֹ מִי יְשׂוֹחֵחַ 53:8
כִּי נִגְזַר מֵאֶרֶץ חַיִּים מִפֶּשַׁע עַמִּי נֶגַע לָמוֹ:

וַיִּתֵּן אֶת־רְשָׁעִים קִבְרוֹ וְאֶת־עָשִׁיר בְּמֹתָיו 53:9
עַל לֹא־חָמָס עָשָׂה וְלֹא מִרְמָה בְּפִיו:

וַיהוָה חָפֵץ דַּכְּאוֹ הֶחֱלִי 53:10
אִם־תָּשִׂים אָשָׁם נַפְשׁוֹ יִרְאֶה זֶרַע יַאֲרִיךְ יָמִים
וְחֵפֶץ יְהוָה בְּיָדוֹ יִצְלָח:

מֵעֲמַל נַפְשׁוֹ יִרְאֶה יִשְׂבָּע בְּדַעְתּוֹ 53:11
יַצְדִּיק צַדִּיק עַבְדִּי לָרַבִּים וַעֲוֹנֹתָם הוּא יִסְבֹּל:

לָכֵן אֲחַלֶּק־לוֹ בָרַבִּים וְאֶת־עֲצוּמִים יְחַלֵּק שָׁלָל 53:12
תַּחַת אֲשֶׁר הֶעֱרָה לַמָּוֶת נַפְשׁוֹ וְאֶת־פֹּשְׁעִים נִמְנָה
וְהוּא חֵטְא־רַבִּים נָשָׂא וְלַפֹּשְׁעִים יַפְגִּיעַ: ס

52:13 Behold, My servant will prosper, He will be high and lifted up and greatly exalted.

14 Just as many were astonished at you, so His appearance was marred more than any man and His form more than the sons of men.

15 Thus He will sprinkle many nations, kings will shut their mouths on account of Him; for what had not been told them they will see, and what they had not heard they will understand.

53:1 Who has believed our message? And to whom has the arm of the LORD been revealed?

2 For He grew up before Him like a tender shoot, and like a root out of parched ground; He has no stately form or majesty that we should look upon Him, nor appearance that we should be attracted to Him.

3 He was despised and forsaken of men, a man of sorrows and acquainted with grief; and like one from whom men hide their face He was despised, and we did not esteem Him.

4 Surely our griefs He Himself bore, And our sorrows He carried; yet we ourselves esteemed Him stricken, smitten of God, and afflicted.

5 But He was pierced through for our transgressions, He was crushed for our iniquities; the chastening for our well being fell upon Him, and by His scourging we are healed.

6 All of us like sheep have gone astray, each of us has turned to his own way; but the LORD has caused the iniquity of us all to fall on Him.

7 He was oppressed and He was afflicted, yet He did not open His mouth; like a lamb that is led to slaughter, and like a sheep that is silent before its shearers, so He did not open His mouth.

8 By oppression and judgment He was taken away; and as for His generation, who considered that He was cut off out of the land of the living for the transgression of my people, to whom the stroke was due?

9 His grave was assigned with wicked men, yet He was with a rich man in His death, because He had done no violence, nor was there any deceit in His mouth.

10 But the LORD was pleased to crush Him, putting Him to grief; if He would render Himself as a guilt offering, He will see His offspring, He will prolong His days, and the good pleasure of the LORD will prosper in His hand.

11 As a result of the anguish of His soul, He will see it and be satisfied; by His knowledge the Righteous One, My Servant, will justify the many, as He will bear their iniquities.

12 Therefore, I will allot Him a portion with the great, and He will divide the booty with the strong; because He poured out Himself to death, and was numbered with the transgressors; yet He Himself bore the sin of many, and interceded for the transgressors.

Other prophecies:

✡ *Isaiah 40:3-5* — "*The voice of one crying in the wilderness: 'Prepare the way of the LORD; Make straight in the desert a highway for our God. Every valley shall be exalted and every mountain and hill brought low; The crooked places shall be made straight and the rough places smooth; the glory of the LORD shall be revealed, and all flesh shall see it together; for the mouth of the LORD has spoken.'*"

✡ *Isaiah 40:9-10* — "*O Zion, You who bring good tidings, Get up into the high mountain; O Jerusalem, You who bring good tidings, Lift up your voice with strength, Lift it up, be not afraid; Say to the cities of Judah, 'Behold your God!' Behold, the LORD God shall come with strength, and His arm shall rule for Him; Behold, His reward is with Him, And His work before Him.*"

✡ *Isaiah 2:3-5* — "*Many people shall come and say, 'Come, and let us go up to the mountain of the LORD, to the house of the God of Jacob; He will teach us His ways, and we shall walk in His paths.' For out of Zion shall go forth the law, and the word of the LORD from Jerusalem. He shall judge between the nations, and rebuke many people; they shall beat their swords into plowshares, and their spears into pruning hooks; nation shall not lift up sword against nation, neither shall they learn war anymore. O house of Jacob, come and let us walk in the light of the LORD.*"

✡ *Malachi 3:1* — "*'Behold, I send My messenger, and he will prepare the way before Me. And the Lord, whom you seek, will suddenly come to His temple, even the Messenger of the covenant, in whom you delight. Behold, He is coming,' says the LORD of hosts.*"

✡ *Isaiah 33:17, 21-22* — "*Your eyes will see the King in His beauty. But there the majestic LORD will be for us a place of broad rivers and streams. For the LORD is our Judge, the LORD is our Lawgiver, the LORD is our King; He will save us.*"

✡ *Daniel 7:13-14* — "*I was watching in the night visions, and behold, One like the Son of Man, coming with the clouds of heaven! He came to the Ancient of Days, and they brought Him near before Him. Then to Him was given dominion and glory and a kingdom that all peoples, nations, and languages should serve Him. His dominion is an everlasting dominion, which shall not pass away, and His kingdom the one which shall not be destroyed.*"

✡ *Psalm 110:1* —*"The* LORD *said to my Lord, 'Sit at My right hand, till I make Your enemies Your footstool.'"*

✡ *Zechariah 12:10* —*"And I will pour on the house of David and on the inhabitants of Jerusalem the Spirit of grace and supplication; then they will look on Me whom they pierced. Yes, they will mourn for Him as one mourns for his only son, and grieve for Him as one grieves for a firstborn."*

✡ *Zechariah 14:3-4* —*"Then the* LORD *will go forth and fight against those nations, as He fights in the day of battle. And in that day His feet will stand on the Mount of Olives, which faces Jerusalem on the east."*

✡ *Zechariah 14:9,16* — *"And the* LORD *shall be King over all the earth. In that day it shall be -- `The* LORD *is one', And His name one. And it shall come to pass that everyone who is left of all the nations which came against Jerusalem shall go up from year to year to worship the King, the* LORD *of hosts, and to keep the Feast of Tabernacles."*

✡ *Job 19:25-27* —*"For I know that my Redeemer lives, and He shall stand at last on the earth; and after my skin is destroyed, this I know, that in my flesh I shall see God, Whom I shall see for myself, and my eyes shall behold, and not another. How my heart yearns within me!"*

✡ *Proverbs 30:4* —*"Who has ascended into heaven, or descended? Who has gathered the wind in His fists? Who has bound the waters in a garment? Who has established all the ends of the earth? What is His name, and what is His Son's name, surely you know?"*

For Further Reading

On general matters of prophecy and theology:

Answering Jewish Objections to Jesus, Vol. 1-5, by Michael Brown. An engaging and personal series of in-depth reflections on a nearly exhaustive set of objections to the Messianic faith.

Messianic Christology by Arnold Fructenbaum.

What the Rabbis Know About the Messiah by Rachmiel Frydland

On the suffering of Messiah:

The Death of Messiah, edited by Kai Kjaer-Hansen, a compilation of articles (including one by the present author) which consider the Messiah' suffering in light of contemporary Lubavitch (Chabad) Hasidism, whose late Rabbi is believed by some to be the Messiah.

The Servant of Jehovah by David Baron, gives a great overview on Isaiah 53 in the context of Isaiah 40-66.

A Hebrew Christian looks at Isaiah 53 by Sanford Mills. Out of print, but a useful overview of the portion.

The Sufferings and the Glories of the Messiah by John Brown, Baker Book House. A deeply devotional look at the Messiah's sufferings for our sins.

On the area of Messiah's nature by a variety of Jewish believers:

Rays of Messiah's Glory and *Zechariah* by David Baron. Baron always wrote with his finger on the text and his eye on our people to clearly show from the Scriptures that Yeshua is the Messiah and Lord of Israel.

The Life and Times of Jesus the Messiah by Alfred Edersheim. A comprehensive study of the Gospels in its Jewish frame of reference with particular attention given to many of the rabbinical opinions regarding Messiah. Here is a section looking at Isaiah 53 that may be helpful.

Messianic Prophecy in the Old Testament by Aaron Kligerman is in some ways a simpler book than the others, but also gives some rabbinical referencing as well as a comprehensive overview of the major messianic prophecies in their historical context.

The Messiahship of Jesus: What Jews and Jewish Christians Say by Arthur W. Kac is a compendium of various viewpoints about Yeshua by numerous non-believing and believing Jewish writers.

More Discipleship Materials from Word of Messiah

1. *Messiah in the Feasts of Israel* - Eye-opening! The meaning of the Biblical feasts in light of the New Covenant: Passover, Firstfruits, Shavuot, Trumpets, Yom Kippur, Sukkot, Hanukkah, Purim and more! (232 pp.)

2. *Even You Can Share The Jewish Messiah!* - A short booklet with key information on sharing Yeshua with friends and neighbors, even "to the Jew first" (Romans 1:16). (28 pp.)

3. *The Messianic Answer Book* - Answers to the 14 most asked questions Jewish people have about The Faith. Excellent tool for sharing with those seeking answers! (112 pp.)

4. *Messianic Wisdom: Practical Scriptural Answers for Your Life* - Get a grasp on Messianic Jewish issues and living out your faith in Messiah. Essential and inspiring, this book is for every growing disciple of Yeshua! (200 pp.)

5. *The Messianic Passover Haggadah* - The perfect guide for conducting your own Passover Seder, for family or congregational use, or to simply learn more about Messiah and Passover. (40 pp.)

6. *Messianic Life Lessons from the Book of Ruth* - an in-depth, information-rich devotional commentary on what is a priceless book of restoration from the Tanakh. (248 pp.)

7. *Messianic Life Lessons from the Book of Jonah: Finding and Following the Will of God* - Do you want to know God's will for your life? Jonah proves this will not help! A slender, wonderful commentary on this book about Israel's mission to the Gentiles. (154 pp.)

8. *Honoring God with My Life: Issues of Sense and Sensibility* by Miriam Nadler, this expositional study of Titus 2:3-5 is perfect for women's studies and all those seeking to live out God's purpose. (200 pp.)

9. *Abiding in Messiah - Bearing Fruit in Yeshua.* In this book by Miriam Nadler you will learn what matters most to God and discover a life of significance through abiding in Messiah. (118 pp.)

Glossary of Jewish Terms

AFIKOMEN: piece of *matzah* that is hidden during a Passover meal, to be found and eaten at the third cup.

AGGADAH (also *haggadah* or "telling"): sections of Talmud and Midrash containing homiletic expositions of Bible, legends, and stories from tradition. Also may refer to a booklet used to go through a Passover seder, such as *The Messianic Passover Haggadah*.

ANI MA'AMIN ("I believe"): name given to Maimonides' Thirteen Principles of Faith (*Sheloshah-Asar Ikkarim*), which attempt to set out the basic beliefs of Judaism as understood during the Middle Ages. Remains fundamental for traditional Judaism until today.

AVODAH ("worship"): service to God, originally applied to Temple service. Literally means "work."

BRIT CHADASHAH (also *habrit hachadasha*, "New Covenant"): the Apostolic Writings, often called the "New Testament." The term is from Jeremiah 31:31. See Appendix A.

BRIT MILAH ("covenant of circumcision"): ceremony of circumcision performed upon Jewish males on the eighth day. Traditionally performed by a *mohel*. This ceremony is also called a *bris*.

GEMARA ("completion"): the final layer of commentary of the Talmud, commenting on the Mishnah, compiled up to 500 CE.

HALAKHAH ("walking"): Traditional Jewish law.

HANUKKAH ("dedication"): Feast commemorating the rebuilding and dedication of the Temple after its desecration by Syrian invaders. Referenced in the books of extra-Biblical books of Maccabees and in John 10:22. From the verb *hanakh* or "train," used for a disciple.

HASHEM ("the Name"): a reverent and traditional way of referring to God. It refers specifically to his four-letter Personal Name, rendered in many English Bibles as "Lord," called the "tetragrammaton" (**י** *yud*, **ה** *hey*, **ו** *vav*, **ה** *hey; note: Hebrew is written right to left*).

HASIDISM (from *hasid*, meaning "pious one"): Movement of Judaism started in the 18th century by Rabbi Israel Baal Shem Tov, with emphasis on personal piety and mysticism, against the intellectual approach of their opponents (who were also Orthodox). They are characterized today by devotion to a *Rebbe* (or dynastic spiritual leader of the community), emphasis on learning, and traditional dress. Often named by town of origin (for example, Lubavitch).

KABBALAH ("receiving"): Jewish mysticism. Beginning with Oral Traditions since 2nd Temple destruction (70 CE), and culminating in the medieval mystical text called the *Zohar.* Figures prominently into Hasidic Judaism.

KAVANAH ("intentionality"): a traditional concept regarding how one is to pray to God. It speaks of being focused and not distracted; purposeful and not haphazard; fervent and not apathetic; reverent and not insolent.

KETUVIM ("Writings"): the third section of the Hebrew Bible (after *Torah* and *Nevi'im*).

MAIMONIDES: Rabbi Moshe ben Maimon (traditionally called by the acrostic "the RaMbaM"), the renowned Jewish teacher, philosopher, and physician, 1135-1204 CE.

MASHIACH ("Anointed," Greek *christos* or "Christ"): Messiah, the Anointed of God to bring salvation to humanity. See Lessons 1, 2, 8 and 9.

MATZAH ("unleavened bread"): bread made without yeast.

MAZEL TOV ("good fortune"): phrase of Yiddish origin (*maze*l tav), from earlier Rabbinic Hebrew which is used today in Israel (maz*al* tov). Said at weddings, etc., to mean "congratulations."

MEGILLOT ("Scrolls," plural of *megillah*): A grouping of Scriptures found within Ketuvim, each of which is traditionally read on various holiday: Song of Songs (read on Passover, or, in some communities, at the onset of Shabbat), Ruth (Shavuot), Lamentations (Tisha B'Av), Ecclesiastes (Sukkot), and Esther (Purim).

MIDRASH ("teaching," plural *midrashim*): Method of interpreting Scripture to elucidate legal points or bring out lessons through stories. Also a designation of post-Talmud rabbinical literature.

MIDRASH RABBAH: A compilation of *Midrashim* on the Torah and Megillot extending from 5th to 12th century. Often divided according to the specific book, e.g. Deuteronomy Rabbah.

MIKVEH ("reservoir" or "collected water"): ceremonial cleansing for ritual purification, and thus it became a word often used by many Messianic believers to refer to believers immersion or *tevilah*.

MISHNAH ("repetition"): Legal codification of basic Jewish Law, and foundational to later Rabbinic Judaism. Compiled by Judah Ha-Nasi around 200CE. With Gemara, it makes up the Talmud.

NEVI'IM ("prophets"): the second of three sections of the Hebrew Bible, falling between *Torah* and *Ketuvim*.

PASSOVER (Hebrew, *Pesach*): Foundational biblical holiday commemorating the rescue of the children of Israel from Egypt, and pointing to the sacrificial death of Messiah.

PURIM ("lots"): Holiday based on the book of Esther, often celebrated by giving gifts, dressing in costumes, and a dramatic reenactment of the story (a Purim play).

RASHI: Rabbi Shlomo Yitzchaki, famous for his foundational Rabbinic exegesis, 1040-1105CE.

ROSH HASHANAH ("head of the year"): Traditional Jewish New Year stemming from the Feast of Trumpets in Leviticus 23. See also Yom Teruah.

RUACH HAKODESH ("the Holy Spirit"): the Person Who is God and applies God's plan of redemption to the life of the believer. See Lessons 11 and 12. (*Ruach* = Spirit, breath, or wind)

SEDER ("order"): a structured meal celebrated usually on one of the first two nights of Passover. See *The Messianic Passover Haggadah*.

SHAVUOT ("weeks," in Greek, *Pentecost*): Holiday known as the "Season of the Giving of the Law," also when the spirit of God was given to believers in Yeshua.

SUKKOT ("booths," plural of *sukkah*): Feast to remember God's provision and protection in the wilderness wanderings, celebrated by creating and living in makeshift dwellings for eight days.

TALMIDUT ("discipleship"): the process of becoming a *talmid* (student or disciple). A similar concept, *hanukkah*, from *hanakh*, is mentioned in Lesson 1 but connotes "training" or "dedication."

TALMUD ("study"): The primary written corpus of the "Oral Law." Made up of Mishnah and Gemara, there is both a Babylonian and Jerusalem Talmud, with the Babylonian Talmud being much larger and carrying more authority. Compiled from 200-500CE.

TANAKH: The Hebrew Bible, coming from an acrostic of its parts: *Torah* (Pentateuch), *Nevi'im*, and *Ketuvim* (Writings). Tanakh is pronounced with a rough "ch" sound (as in the Scottish *loch*) because "K" (kaf) changes in the middle of a syllable or end of a word. See Appendix A for two orders of the books of the Hebrew Bible.

TARGUM ("translation"): traditional Aramaic paraphrase of Scriptures, written between 100 BCE- 100 CE

TEVILAH ("immersion"): the practice of plunging believers into water as a symbolic testimony of their identification with Messiah.

TORAH: Divine Instruction. Also refers to the Five Books of Moses (or Pentateuch), and sometimes referred to as the Law, due to appearance of Mosaic Law in this portion of the Hebrew Bible.

YESHU: an acrostic meaning *yemach shmo vezichro*, or "may His name be blotted out forever," often used as a corruption, or to avoid saying the Hebrew name *Yeshua*.

YESHUA: the Hebrew name often transliterated through the Greek as "Jesus," meaning "the Lord is salvation," or "the Lord saves."

YOM TERUAH ("day of blasting," or the Feast of Trumpets): A mysterious holiday found in Leviticus 23:24, this day begins the High Holy Days and Fall Feasts, and prophetically points to the catching up (or "rapture") of believers.

YOM KIPPUR ("day of atonement"): found in Leviticus 23:27-32, and simply called "the fast" in Acts 27:9, this close of the High Holy Days is considered the holiest day of the year in traditional Judaism. It points to the time of Israel's national repentance to Messiah (Zechariah 12:10).

ZIKKARON ("remembrance"): the practice of eating *matzah* and red wine or grape juice (based on the *Afikomen* and third cup of a traditional seder) so as to remember Yeshua's sacrifice.

NOTES

NOTES

Word of Messiah Ministries

P. O. Box 79238

Charlotte, NC 28271

Phone: 704-544-1948

Email: info@wordofmessiah.org

www.wordofmessiah.org